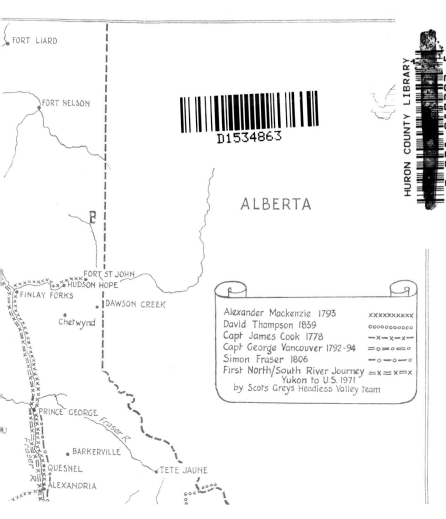

FORT LIARD

FORT NELSON

ALBERTA

D1534863

FORT ST JOHN
HUDSON HOPE
FINLAY FORKS
DAWSON CREEK
Chetwynd

Alexander Mackenzie 1793	xxxxxxxxxx
David Thompson 1859	ooooooooooo
Capt James Cook 1778	—x—x—x—
Capt George Vancouver 1792-94	=o=o=o
Simon Fraser 1806	—o—o—o
First North/South River Journey	=x=x=x
Yukon to U.S. 1971 by Scots Greys Headless Valley team	

PRINCE GEORGE
Fraser R.
Fraser
BARKERVILLE
QUESNEL
ALEXANDRIA
TETE JAUNE

140204

917.11   Fiennes, Sir Ranulph, bart., 1944-
Fie   The Headless Valley. London, Hodder
          and Stoughton, 1973.
             222 p. illus., maps.

          Includes bibliography.

          1. Rivers - British Columbia.
          2. British Columbia - Description and
          travel. I. Title.

                              H-8087
                                M

By the same author

A TALENT FOR TROUBLE
ICE FALL IN NORWAY

THE
HEADLESS VALLEY

by

Ranulph Fiennes

HODDER AND STOUGHTON
LONDON SYDNEY AUCKLAND TORONTO

For Brian Walter—for his knowledge
and kindness which have made
it all possible

The Canyon has been called beautiful.
If this is beauty, it is the beauty of nightmare.
It has been called magnificent, but this is the
magnificence of destruction.
It has been called sublime, and so it is, with the
sublimity of blind and senseless force.

from *The Fraser* by Bruce Hutchison

Foreword

by

HIS ROYAL HIGHNESS
THE DUKE OF KENT

IT CANNOT BE VERY OFTEN NOWADAYS THAT ANY EXPLORER CAN genuinely claim to have achieved a 'first': Ranulph Fiennes, who conceived and carried out the Headless Valley expedition, already has at least two to his credit and no doubt at this very moment the seeds of one or two future enterprises are germinating in his mind.

One's first thought on hearing about such an adventure as this one is that only foolhardy madmen would attempt such a thing, and the reaction of the Commanding Officer who agreed to release any of his soldiers 'mad enough to volunteer' is probably that of most responsible men. The success of the expedition, however, somewhat belies this theory, and one of the lessons to come out of this and all similarly hazardous exploits is that without the most meticulous planning and preparation they literally have not a hope of success.

But all the planning and all the most sophisticated equipment are of precious little use without the skill to get the best out of them, and above all without the leadership that persuades men to go on enduring horrors which all their instincts have long ago told them are unbearable.

Fortunately there are, and I am sure always will be, people who have the right combination of restlessness, curiosity and courage to make them seek out challenges and then overcome them. The rest of us may have to be content with hearing or reading about it, but at least we can enjoy some vicarious excitement by reading as lively and vivid an account as this one. Not only is it told with a dry wit, but if anything the rigours of this remarkable journey have been understated. I am very happy to know that among many other organisations and individuals who contributed to the expedition's success were the Royal National Life-Boat Institution and the Royal Scots Dragoon Guards.

I am therefore delighted to be able to salute the achievement of Ranulph Fiennes and his team in their conquest of the Headless Valley.

Edward

Contents

Illustrations

Acknowledgment
* Bryn Campbell, *Observer*

Maps

I

Far Below London

ONE OF THE LAST GREAT TRACTS OF VIRGIN WILDERNESS LEFT ON
this earth: a land of primeval forest and bleak swamp traversed by
turbulent fast-flowing rivers, not ordinary rivers but thousands of
miles of the roughest inland water in the world. Rivers which
thunder over jagged rocks, hurtle between deep-cleft canyons
greater than the Colorado Canyon, with whipping whirlpools and
tearing rapids and somewhere in their midst the mighty Nahanni
Falls, more than twice the height of Niagara. To hear that this great
untrammelled vastness existed was a challenge in itself; to learn
that the most rugged region of Western Canada might be crossed
from end to end by boat but that this had not yet been accomplished,
made it irresistible. But how to do it, how to get there, that was the
problem.

I had heard tales of the area all my life, for both my father and
grandfather had been to British Columbia. My great-uncle had
inherited the family title and estate and so my grandfather took to a
life of wandering, from South Africa to the Seychelles, from Alberta
to the Leeward Islands, even spending time as a penniless fur-
trapper in the sub-Arctic. When the half-breed Plains Indians of
Western Canada has risen against the Government's settlements
policies in 1885 he had left his trapline and signed on with the
North West Mounted Police. He had had a number of amazing
adventures before he eventually left Canada and had regaled my

father with them in his youth so that as soon as he got the opportunity, my father too had gone straight to Canada. He had passed on his tales of adventure, and those of his father, to my mother so that although my father was killed in the war just before I was born, I had still heard from my mother about 'out west'. The early explorers of a hundred years ago had struggled up many of the rivers but none of them had completed the greatest and most rewarding journey of all, through that most rugged and beautiful region, the mountain massif of British Columbia, travelling from the Yukon border over the intercontinental divide and down the turbulent Fraser River to the Pacific and the 49th Parallel.

All one winter I mulled over the possibilities. Perhaps an overland winter Arctic expedition ending in the Yukon so that all the bulky equipment could be brought back to civilisation in spring by boat, or maybe I could venture forth for a year alone exploring by boat or ski, sled or on foot according to the season of the year. We were spending the winter in a small cottage on the western side of Loch Maree, well north of Inverness. Away from the telephone, mail and friends, I plotted and planned ways and means of getting to western Canada.

One day a telegram arrived; Cubby Broccoli, the film wizard, was apparently searching diligently all over Britain for a new 007 for the next James Bond film. After Sean Connery's temporary abdication, and George Lazenby's equally temporary occupation, the directors were now looking for a 'young English gentleman type'. For some very obscure reason an actors' agency had thought that I might fit the bill.

Once they had promised to pay the return fare to London, I agreed to meet Broccoli and went south. The interview lasted ten minutes, sufficient for them to decide that I was too young, most unBondlike, and facially more like a farmhand than 'an English gentleman'.

However, the journey was not fruitless for I bumped into an old friend in the Royal Scots Greys and over a drink told him that I was thinking of going to the Canadian Arctic, could I but think of a way to finance an expedition. Shortly afterwards, a letter came from the Scots Greys Headquarters with a most unusual proposal.

On an earlier expedition by mini-hovercraft up the Nile, I had had an ex-paratrooper turned Gillette salesman in the crew. His efforts to sell razor blades to bearded Arabs had met with little success, so after our journey he had decided to rejoin the Army. Later, as a Captain in the Scots Greys, he had thought up an ambitious 'adventure training' scheme called Exercise Arctic Moose.

Harold Wilson was at the time pruning the Army and the Scots Greys were shortly to amalgamate with another regiment. Before they lost their traditional identity and their grey berets, they were naturally keen to have one or two last flings; so Arctic Moose was welcomed and its prospectus sent off to the Canadian Army for approval.

The scheme was basically to be a race from Vancouver up the Fraser and Peace Rivers to the Barren Lands and thence to Yellow-knife in the North West Territories. The teams selected from all the armies of the western bloc, would cover the 2,000-mile route by canoe, pack-horse and *langlauf* ski.

The Arctic Moose papers were sent back by the Canadian authorities with an accompanying report from the Northern Region Headquarters of their National Defence Department.

They didn't believe that 'the author of Arctic Moose appreciates fully the enormity of such an undertaking. It may indeed involve only 2,000 miles of travel but the going is quite unlike anything to be found in the British Isles or anywhere else. The Fraser from above Hope to a little south of Lillooet must be seen to be believed; even Simon Fraser himself couldn't paddle down it. Another problem is blackfly and other assorted insects; hundreds of billions of them. Furthermore there will be serious trouble with navigation and countless portages over muskeg.'

The letter made it clear that Arctic Moose was not feasible but it also suggested an alternative scheme.

On July 20th, 1871, British Columbia, a vast mountain mass (large enough to accommodate some twenty Switzerlands and all of Great Britain) joined the Canadian Confederation. By this union Canada became a transcontinental Dominion stretching from the Pacific to the Atlantic. The Province was to celebrate its centenary throughout 1971 with activities to commemorate various historic events. They would welcome an army expedition from the 'old country' to retrace the remarkable journeys of the British Columbian pioneers, but these routes were hazardous, and none could be completed without many weeks of hard travel, for the rivers and terrain had changed little if at all during the century which had elapsed since the pioneering days.

The Scots Greys were overworked with squadrons in Ireland, Cyprus and the Middle East: there were no officers and few soldiers to spare for any such lengthy expedition as the Canadians suggested. But they were determined to follow up the matter and, since I was on the regiment's reserve strength, they sent me the Arctic Moose file with the promise that they would provide 'two or three soldiers and some supplies' if I came up with a reasonable scheme.

Obviously it would need more than two or three soldiers and some supplies to achieve such a journey but at least they would be a start and with army backing it shouldn't be difficult to get RAF transport to and from Canada. But where would the money come from? Money for the expensive and varied equipment which was bound to be needed and which the Army could not supply, as I knew from past expeditions. I would have to obtain everything on loan from the manufacturers, and they would only help if assured of maximum publicity. Also the expedition must be filmed, and sponsored by a national newspaper, otherwise I could not afford to spend five months organising it and probably another five in Canada.

First I must find a job in London to keep the family kettle boiling whilst I organised the expedition, then I must try to persuade the Army that my proposed trip to Canada was heavily sponsored by a number of large British companies whilst at the same time assuring the companies that the Army were in it up to their eyeballs. Both statements moreover would need to be true for it would only need either side to get cold feet for the whole expedition to crumble.

I telephoned the Colonel of the Royal Scots Greys in Edinburgh and he agreed to let me select three men from the only squadron still in Britain. So on my way south to look for a job I called in at Redford Barracks in Edinburgh. The Colonel kindly said that I could pick anyone 'mad enough to volunteer' but this was not as simple as it sounded for less than a third of the regiment were in Britain and those present were mostly married or in sedentary administrative positions.

Bearing in mind that we should later want rations and other stores from the Quartermaster, I paid him a visit. Major Bill Haynes had been in the regiment with my father in the last war but he knew me of old as a 'compulsive scrounger of stores' and cocked a wary eye when he saw me. He was as helpful as he could be but much of the regimental equipment was abroad or ready for signing over prior to amalgamation.

Coming out of his office, I met one of his corporals, an Edinburgh Scotsman called Joseph Skibinski. He had joined our regimental cross-country ski team which trained in the Bavarian mountains for three months each winter. One Christmas the two of us tried to reach the summit of the lofty Wertach-horn. A blizzard blew up whilst we were a couple of hundred feet from the peak. We reached the top, narrowly avoiding precipitation over the edge by the gale and then, on the way down, found that our hands were numb and quite useless. Luckily we found an old forester's cabin just above the tree line. We broke in through an iced-up window and spent a very merry Christmas Eve with a bottle of cherry brandy and some playing cards. I came to know and like Skibinski and, seeing him of a sudden in Edinburgh, he seemed a natural choice for the Canadian journey. I explained to him in lurid detail the probable route we would be attempting, admitting that better men than we had tried it but none had to date succeeded.

Skibinski volunteered at once. He said he was married with two young children but that 'Suzanne willna mind. She kens I like that sort of thing.' For a long while we discussed other soldiers who might volunteer and he mentioned young Jack McConnell, whom I remembered vaguely as an athletic member of the ski team. He too was married, though only twenty-one, and his wife was about to increase the McConnell clan 'with a wee lad they'll call Jason', Skibinski confidently predicted.

Trooper McConnell appeared from nowhere as though summoned by bush telegraph and was immediately eager to join the expedition, though somewhat dubious as to his wife's philosophy about such activities.

Corporal Skibinski and McConnell were both good radio operators, McConnell being a Grade I Signaller. Neither of them were fully trained vehicle mechanics nor medical orderlies, but Skibinski knew of a REME corporal, attached to the Scots Greys, who was a fully trained medic, a mechanic, and extremely fit to boot. This seemed too good to be true but we traced the man down in the greasy bowels of an armoured car's engine compartment. Corporal Stanley Cribbett was a soft-spoken Devon man in his late twenties. He was shy of manner and, although obviously delighted with the prospect of joining us, said he would think it over for a while. I felt there were few things he would do without first summing the situation up carefully.

In London I set about getting a job and had the luck to be chosen by Brian Branston, BBC2's director of Travel and Exploration for a part in his new documentary film on the London sewers and other hidden byways which he was making for his 'World About Us' series. He had chosen Douglas Botting for the main part, a writer who knew a surprising amount about London, above and below pavement level, and Liz Fraser, the vivacious Cockney actress of 'Carry On' fame to inject a modicum of comedy and sensuousness into the sewers. It seemed an interesting if curious way of earning a living under London whilst getting the expedition together.

For the most part I found film work anything but glamorous, in or out of sewers, and it seemed to involve a great deal of very hard work. Nor was my mind set on filming, for the lure of Canada was growing as the dearth of information about British Columbia became increasingly apparent. My wife, Ginnie, went to the Royal Geographical Society, The Royal Commonwealth Society and The Commonwealth Institute and buried herself amongst their musty corridors. For two months she hibernated in numerous libraries, scribbling furiously and checking details from notes of early explorers against the maps I had borrowed from the Army, 200 pounds in weight of four-inches-to-the-mile sheets. We sent enquiring letters to various authorities in Western Canada and contacted both the British Museum and the Royal Zoological Society who agreed to sponsor the expedition. The former wanted a number of fossils from the rarely visited northern Rockies and the latter were eager to obtain specimens of the Least Weasel, the smallest member of the weasel tribe.

By mid-February, Ginnie's researches had revealed that despite the plethora of rivers throughout British Columbia there was only one possible north-south route and that was down the Rocky Mountain Trench. This is the name given to the valley-rift in the midst of the Rocky Mountains into which most of the rivers of the area find their way. But right across the middle of the Trench was a giant hummock known as the Sifton Pass. To the north of this the river systems of the Trench flowed northwards and, to the south, the rivers flowed south all the way to Finlay Forks and Pine Pass where the Rockies are cleft by a spectacular canyon. Our route then would be *up* the Kechika River against the current to its source, where we would portage over the riveraine divide by way of the Sifton Pass at 3,273 feet. From the Pass itself a stream called the Tochieka or Fox appeared to struggle south through swamp and forest to the Finlay River. Once on the Finlay we would travel south with the current but not for good for we would still have to push our way *up* the Parsnip, Pack and Crooked Rivers to Summit Lake. One more short footslog on land and then at last we would be on the Fraser which rushes south into the Pacific at Vancouver.

The journey from border to border covers 900 miles as the crow flies. As the rivers flow, perhaps a third of that distance again can be added to the total mileage. Rapids and cataracts characterised most of the rivers and reports describing them are spattered with accounts of boats disappearing in whirlpools and rock-battered bodies reappearing as so much pulp in the eddies below. Of the Kechika and Fox Rivers however we could find no descriptions or reports at all. A French explorer had once attempted the Sifton Pass from the south using pack-horses, specially-made riverboats and Citroën half-tracks. He had struggled north for many weeks finally admitting defeat and abandoning the equipment not far beyond the Pass.

Then some replies to my letters started to arrive. The Director of Mapping sent 1:250,000 scale maps of the Kechika and Fox Rivers and the official Government reports on the region, which I noticed were dated 1891 and 1914. One map showed a dotted line which ran beside the Kechika and Fox south to the Finlay. Did that dotted line mean that there had once been a trail over the Sifton Pass and if so, would it still be possible to find it? There appeared to be no sign of human habitation in the whole vast area of mountain and forest around the Sifton.

A letter came from Mr Ron Jones of British Columbia's Timber Land Service, a man who knew as much as anyone about the country's interior. He had spoken to the Centenary's Provincial Officer who was convinced that we would 'not be able to complete that which we had presently set out'. He observed that

> conditions in the backwoods can change quite quickly so that accurate information is impossible to obtain. This is a very civilised country, so long as you keep on the highway. Five miles off it you could be in West Africa. Should a Black Bear (numerous in all regions) become too friendly around your camp, it should be shot . . . the hind legs are good eating. A grizzly should never be shot unless actually attacking. A full-grown grizzly can only be stopped by a neck shot, the rest of him is like a Sherman tank . . . Only the 'dry belt' rattle snake is poisonous . . . A big problem is the flying bugs, large mosquitoes, no-see-ums and several types of large black flies. Also the deer tick which digs its head deep into your flesh which you will not usually feel until it is half full of blood. In the Rockies it can cause a fever and must be dug out with a knife for it is very difficult to remove the two foremost legs . . .

Officers from the northern stations of the Mounties—RCMP is the local term—wrote with further disturbing information. Inspector Webster of the Prince George Sub-Division stated, 'Unfortunately

I cannot supply further information about the conditions of the rivers you hope to traverse . . . Whenever the necessity arises for members of our Force to proceed into the areas in question, this is always done by aircraft.'

He also remarked that much of the Parsnip and Finlay Rivers were now an enormous man-made lake, 250 miles long. This had been caused by a dam on the Peace River. The lake was subject to tidal waves caused by landslides and sudden storms with waves of eight feet or more. This was especially unpleasant due to the millions of huge floating logs which jammed much of the lake's surface. The banks too were usually inaccessible in a storm, since the forests flanking the lake were themselves partially submerged. Many hundreds of moose and a number of Indians had already been drowned in this nightmarish water.

*   *   *

March came with little enough time left if the expedition was to be through the Rockies before winter. It was not too easy arranging the hundred and one small details necessary to launch an expedition whilst wandering around in the London sewers.

All I needed was a telephone and some time off, but the camera teams were busy all day and telephones were scarce in the London sewer system though—judging by Alf, our sewer-guide's, remarks— one could find almost anything else down there, from false teeth to escaped pet alligators.

From the sewers we moved to the GPO tunnels and here there was no shortage of underground telephones from which to chat up the many companies making the expedition equipment we would need. By this time I could promise the Publicity and Advertising Officer of each firm that his support would not be one-sided since my literary agent, George Greenfield, had obtained a contract with the *Observer* newspaper. They would be sending their top photographer, Bryn Campbell, on the expedition. He was a former Photographer of the Year and a seasoned traveller. Furthermore the BBC Travel and Exploration Department liked the idea of the journey and were hoping to send a two-man film team with us. For reasons I was none too sure about, they declared that, whatever craft we used, they would bring with them an experienced Royal National Lifeboat Institution crewman to man their boat whilst they were filming. The team was increasing; we were now eight in number; ten counting my wife Ginnie and a REME corporal who were to drive the vehicles of our road support group.

There was an ancient Land-Rover which had seen service in Aden, Cyprus, and Germany. The Army had condemned it as 'Beyond Economical Repair' but it was short-circuited from the knacker's yard and appropriated by the expedition. After many telegrams had flown back and forth between London sewers and the British Defence Liaison Staff in Ottawa, the Canadians finally agreed to provide a 'douze-and-a-half'. With French-Canadian logic this ponderous army lorry can carry about three tons, using a phenomenal amount of fuel.

British Petroleum and Duckhams Oil kindly agreed to sponsor all the fuel requirements, including the transport of heavy 45-gallon drums to isolated parts of British Columbia. By early April some nine thousand pounds' worth of expedition equipment—from radios to chewing gum, from Arctic bedsocks to talcum powder, from automatic pistols to mosquito nets—was stored carefully in our garage, loft and spare bedroom. (A complete list of our sponsors is provided in the appendix on page 208.)

*   *   *

The under-London filming moved from the deep-freeze fish cellar at Billingsgate which was forty degrees below freezing, on to the Silver Vaults. There was no time to change our clothes between locations and the suave officials in the Vaults found our personal smell most offensive judging by their twitching nostrils. For once Liz Fraser wasn't crowded by over-affectionate extras.

There was a free day that week and I visited British Columbia's Government House in Regent Street. The officials were friendly and helpful but, like their counterparts in Canada House, knew very little about the northern half of their homeland. I browsed through their travel information pamphlets and came across a brochure on the northern town of Fort Nelson.

From Fort Nelson [it said] the rivers flow north to the Nahanni River Valley, known as the Headless Valley. Since the early days when two men of an exploration party were found headless on a path in the valley, weird stories have been told of other disappearances. It seems that the heads of these men had been twisted off by brute strength. The bodies were some distance apart: their heads were never found. For years after this, most of the men who insisted in exploring this valley never returned to tell their story. Some day the valley will be thoroughly explored and its secret revealed. Until then it lies hidden, shrouded in mystery in the deep Northland.

Fascinated by the story, I wrote off to Headquarters Canadian Northern Command for more information. Major Sweeney replied on April 8th from Yellowknife in the North West Territories stating:

The Headless Valley to which you refer is in NWT not BC and is described as Deadmen Valley on our aerial maps. It lies between the first and second canyons of the South Nahanni River. I have it on very reasonable authority—from an old sourdough named Albert Faille—that sometime in the early 1900s the headless skeletons of the McLeod brothers were found lying on a gravel wash where Prairie Creek joins the South Nahanni (with a poke of gold beside them). I am also told that others have vanished in that part of the South Nahanni since then, to the tune of thirty-two in all, the most recent three being in 1963.

Another letter came five days later—from the Brigadier-General's Office in Ottawa—saying that any expedition into the Nahanni area would be extremely hazardous at the best of times and certainly could not be attempted before mid-July, by when the spring floods should have subsided.

Meanwhile Ginnie had unearthed a book, *Dangerous River* by Raymond Patterson, a London banker who had emigrated to Canada. He gave a graphic description of a journey up the South Nahanni in 1928 to a remarkable waterfall. To reach the Falls from Fort Nelson, Patterson had travelled along some four hundred miles of wild river through narrow canyons, past bubbling sulphurous springs and even a double sinkhole known as the Devil's Whirlpool.

Patterson's book decided me. To go all the way to Western Canada prepared for river travel and not to visit the Nahanni, examine the Headless Valley with all its legends or see the fabulous waterfall would be criminal. We would mount a two-pronged expedition: first we would get all our gear to Fort Nelson where we would leave Ginnie, the REME corporal and the vehicles. The rest of us would set out from there in July – the earliest month after the ice break-up permitted by the authorities – to travel north down the Nelson and Liard and up the South Nahanni River, through the Headless Valley to the foot of the great waterfall in the North West Territories. The three soldiers and I would return by boat along the same route by which we had come whilst the BBC team would be taken out by air so that they could carry on filming other parts of Canada meanwhile. This part of the expedition would take one month. Once back at Fort Nelson we would load all our gear onto the vehicles and drive north along the Alaska Highway to Watson Lake just over the border in the Yukon. From there we would attempt a complete transnavigation of British Columbia. We would travel by way of the Hyland, Liard and Kechika Rivers, carry all our gear over the Sifton Pass, find the source of the Fox River and then whip *down* the Finlay and Fraser river systems arriving in the Pacific before winter set in and river travel became too dangerous. The name for the whole double expedition would now be Exercise Headless Valley.

* * *

The last few weeks galloped along. Thankfully we paid a last visit to the London sewers and moved to Sir Winston Churchill's War Room, deep in Whitehall and protected by many feet of concrete. Everything was exactly as it had been on Armistice Day, the wall-charts, the great man's desk with its cigar-cutter and bell-push, the practical little bedroom close to the Operations Centre and the bevy of multi-coloured telephones just as they'd been during their busy Battle of Britain days. Unfortunately none of them worked and I had to use a coin-box phone elsewhere.

Everything seemed more or less ready but I was unable to find boats suitable for the arduous journey ahead, and a company prepared to make three craft available at no cost.

We started by testing two 13-foot inflatables in Snake's Tail rapids on the Dee. For the first time the team were assembled — complete but for the BBC's RNLI crewman. The two BBC men were as inscrutable as Chinamen, said little and gave me the feeling that they were most unimpressed by boats and crew alike. The *Observer* photographer on the other hand was a delightful extrovert. I felt sure he would be a great asset but feared only that he would not stand up to discomfort for very long for he was almost fragile in build.

The corporals learned quickly how to steer the inflatables, how to capsize and then right them in rough water, and how to manhandle them down 70-foot sheer waterfalls with minimal risk and effort. They worked well together and showed no fear of the rapids.

Some thirty members of the press and television recorded our practice session at the Snake's Tail and a picture subsequently appeared in the *Manchester Evening News* showing one of the inflatables being overturned in comparatively calm water. A caption stated that the boat had just capsized.

This wasn't exactly good publicity for the makers, who were doubtful anyway whether their boats would withstand the rapids of the Fraser River, and they withdrew their support.

I could sympathise with their point of view but my own predicament was now critical. The BBC team suggested using RNLI inshore rescue boats which were 16-foot inflatables. The Bridlington

RNLI kindly took the team to sea in one such craft and they proved excellent. The RNLI governors would not lend me three, so I visited the manufacturers—RFD Ltd of Godalming. They too were loth to donate any boats but finally agreed to sell me a new craft at a good discount and to donate a six-year-old boat which had been lying in their back yard. I was still short of one boat and, ideally, would have liked to be able to take along an extra one in case of disasters. Then, not long before we were due to leave England, I contacted a small firm in Wiltshire who made a wide selection of inflatables called C-Craft. They agreed to supply two boats without charge, subject to their passing certain rigorous tests. We took one to the south coast, loaded it with 2,000 pounds of gravel and ploughed through a choppy sea without difficulty. Our boat problems were over.

* * *

On a fine day in spring the 'World About Us' filming ended beneath Piccadilly Circus. The BBC cameras were on the roof of the Lillywhites building and we emerged from a manhole bang in the middle of Lower Regent Street's confluence with the Circus. London being London, nobody took any notice.

The filming finished; I was given a desk and two telephones in one of the Defence Ministry's rabbit warrens to help finalise plans before departure. At the opposite desk sat a busy young civil servant whose head was hidden by an enamel teapot with two faded daffodils protruding from its spout.

The great day arrived when the men came to Battersea Bridge in the antique Land-Rover loaded high with equipment. From Sussex—in an old butcher's van—we brought the boats, outboard motors and ancillary kit, all of which was impregnated with the noxious odour of old meat and fish since the rear of the van had resisted our most determined efforts to purify its atmosphere.

There was a five-knot current running in the Thames that afternoon but all the craft made easy headway with full loads. The bigger RFDs proved difficult boats to carry, for they weighed 250 pounds

apiece and Stanley Cribbett was twelve inches shorter than the rest
of us, so that we moved alongside our burden with the lopsided gait
of a camel, slithering in the Thames-side muck which included a
bloated dog's carcass and several dead birds embalmed in oil.

At the last moment the Army confirmed that they could not lend
us trailers for our road support vehicles. After a flurry of phone calls,
a Chester firm—Dixon Bate Trailers—promised us two. More
serious was an overdue letter from the Mounties who had at last
found some information on the Kechika and Fox Rivers. For at
least sixty miles, they said, these rivers were mere streams and only
by portaging all our kit over a hundred miles might we cross the
Sifton Pass.

To portage our inflatables that distance would be unthinkable,
especially since the Mounties added that the old Indian trails beside
the rivers were now overgrown. With no time to be choosey, I
ordered three collapsible kayaks from Twickenham which were
delivered to RAF Lyneham an hour before our VC10 left for
Alberta. Two of the Corporals flew separately in a Hercules with
the Land-Rover, trailers, and 9,000 pounds of equipment.

As we sped over the great frozen rivers of Greenland, Ginnie read
through some of our recent mail, coming across a letter from a Mr
Harridge of Ancoats. He had read of the expedition and sent a
warning to the Ministry of Defence: 'During recent research I have
discovered something strange about the Valley of the South
Nahanni River which may be of some importance to the
expedition. Under no circumstances must they prospect nor
remove minerals from the soil whilst in this valley. Men who
leave the soil of the Valley alone go unharmed; prospectors are
found dead.'

We had also been wryly amused by a cartoon that appeared in a
Canadian newspaper when plans of our journey were first released
in British Columbia. The drawing depicted a group of Scottish
soldiers in bearskin helmets and carrying fixed bayonets, landing in
a dinghy in a wooded valley. All around were hotels, TV aerials and
tourists. A sign over one hotel announced the Headless Valley
Motel, and its manager was busy telling the leader of the group that

he was fully booked up. A grizzly was licking one of the soldiers' bearskins.

On June 28th we arrived at Edmonton in Alberta. The white concrete runway shimmered in the glare and a fine haze haloed the scrub; a myriad mosquitoes awaiting twilight.

2

Welshman Overboard

WITH TWO THOUSAND MILES OF RIVER TRAVEL AHEAD OF US, THERE was no time to be lost touring Edmonton. The Canadian Army lorry awaited us at the airport as did an English major with an elegant conquistador moustache; he had flown from Ottawa to see us on our way and produced a letter from his Colonel wishing us well during the months to come.

We worked late into the night sorting and loading the vehicles and trailers. Every half-hour or so we would pause to apply more insect repellent to our arms and necks, for a gale howled outside and the mosquito world had joined us in the shelter of the hangars.

We left Edmonton behind us, driving towards the Rockies, on our way to Fort Nelson which lay some six hundred miles to the north-west across a sea of rolling prairie. The roads were good but our vehicles slow and by dusk next day we were still in Alberta.

Some twenty million bison roamed these prairies a hundred and fifty years ago. Many were killed by wolves, bears, and the Indians to whom they meant food, clothing, and tents. Thousands of bison were drowned annually when crossing frozen rivers in spring, starved to death when the snow covered their food, and burned in the great fires of the plains. The white man's policy was to destroy the Indians' livelihood through the virtual extinction of the buffalo herds. That this policy succeeded was a tragedy, but the end of the bison was inevitable for agricultural development of the prairies would not have have been possible whilst the great herds roamed free.

We entered British Columbia without knowing it and the heavens reacted to our arrival with a downpour. The 'old girl' as Stanley Cribbett called the Land-Rover, had been equipped with special, but unfortunately defective, windscreen wipers that only worked when operated manually. Stanley would allow no criticism of the vehicle and, perched on an extra cushion, his nose pressed to the windscreen, he drove with one hand, whilst twiddling the wiper endlessly to and fro with the other.

A flat metal housing protected the battery between the two front seats. I was sitting on the housing between Stanley and Ginnie and became alarmed when acid fumes rose between my legs, the battery temperature indicator swung to the danger level, and my backside grew unbearably hot. Ginnie was squirming about her seat in a vain attempt to dodge the various roof-leaks and we agreed to halt for a while before the batteries exploded.

Not far north of Fort St John, the Alaska Highway ran out of paving and became a quagmire. The rain came in fierce hour-long splurges and the vertical curtain of water drummed the packed dirt of the highway into ooze so that deep runnels and potholes lay hidden beneath a veneer of ochre slime.

Close to the Indian Reserve called Sikanni Chief, we stopped wearily at a roadside café. The doughnuts were stale, the coffee brackish but very welcome, and the little restaurant jangled like a Caribbean band as a dozen intermittent roof dribbles collected in, and overflowed from, an assortment of basins strategically placed on the floor by the student manager of the place.

The student had heard about our expedition on his wireless and told us that we would have to stay at Fort Nelson until the floods there abated.

'You'd be askin' fer trouble to put yer rafts on them northern rivers right now 'cos they're up 'n over the banks and tearin' all the trees down. The folks up at Fort Nelson are havin' a load of trouble with their southern bridge 'cos the river's jammed a whole heap of logs up agin the bridge uprights and the jam's gettin' bigger all the

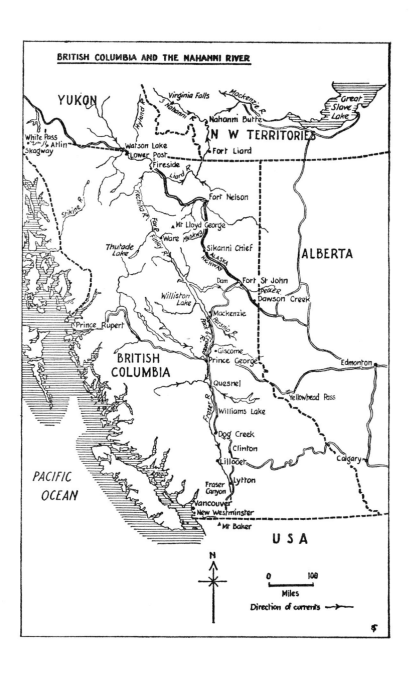

BRITISH COLUMBIA AND THE NAHANNI RIVER

YUKON

Virginia Falls

Mackenzie R.

Great Slave Lake

Nahanni Butte

Nahanni R.

N W TERRITORIES

White Pass
Atlin
Skagway

Watson Lake
Lower Post
Fireside

Fort Liard

Liard R.

Fort Nelson

Stikine R.

Kechika R.

Mt Lloyd George

Fox R.

Ware

Finlay R.

Muskwa R.

Sikanni Chief

Thutade Lake

ALASKA HIGHWAY

ALBERTA

Williston Lake

Dam

Fort St John

Peace R.

Dawson Creek

BRITISH COLUMBIA

Mackenzie

Parsnip R.

Fraser R.

Giscome

Prince George

Prince Rupert

Edmonton

Quesnel

Yellowhead Pass

Williams Lake

Fraser R.

Dog Creek

Clinton

Calgary

Lillooet

Lytton

PACIFIC OCEAN

Fraser Canyon

Vancouver

New Westminster

Mt Baker

USA

N

0   100
Miles

Direction of currents ⟶

ꝸ

time. Won't stand much more pressure, so they say, before the whole goddam bridge goes. Them northern waters are real mean when the big rains come on top of the spring ice run-off. River men with any sense stay home when the Fort Nellie's runnin' wild.'

I asked him about the Nahanni but he'd only heard vague stories of it and wasn't even too sure where the river was.

The rainclouds cleared as we stopped in the canyon of the Sikanni Chief. We had passed two landslides where ragged chunks of the Highway had subsided and fallen into the gorge hundreds of feet below. In these places we hugged the cliff carefully and edged past the void in low gear.

We saw no Indians at Sikanni Chief, an untidy cluster of log cabins and rusting debris. The Sikanni River thundered through the valley heading north-east to join the Fontas and Muskwa. After their union they become the Fort Nelson which itself joins the Liard after cutting north through deep forest for 180 miles. All this water then joins the mighty Mackenzie and empties into the Arctic.

For two hours the Land-Rover's battery acid spat and steamed until the indicator fell back to a safer level and we began the steep climb out of the Sikanni Gorge.

Dusk found us camped in a derelict cabin at Buckinghorse Creek. We found the fishing lines and tempted the creek inmates with doughballs and metal lures. The fish, if there were any, scorned our bait and we dined from army tins. Bully beef on hardtack biscuit was followed by Ginger Pudding—well-known in the last war for its excellent effect on loose bowels. This I could believe since it incapacitated mine for the next two days.

Bryn Campbell was sprouting the beginnings of a fine beard. His good humour was infectious despite the rain and the alarming rumours of the river conditions. He named our cabin Buckinghorse Palace and sang unintelligible ditties which he said were Welsh— and who were we to doubt his word?

At noon on July 2nd the forests fell away from the Highway and the giant stack of Fort Nelson's gas-scrubbing plant, the largest in the world, reared skywards belching poisonous fumes of carbon

Not every river would be plain sailing . . . Boating training in Wales.

Ready for departure at Battersea Bridge; from the left, Joe Skibinski, Jack McConnell, Stanley Cribbett, Corporal Wallace, the author, Bryn Campbell, Ginnie Fiennes

Repairing battered propellers at
Nahanni Butte, Ben, Stanley
and the author.

The seventy channels of the
Splits — which way to go?

and sulphur into the upper atmosphere. Fort Nelson is to gas, say the locals, what the Middle East is to oil.

The first trading outpost in this area was built by a trader called Wilhelm Wenzel in 1805 and named in honour of the victor of Trafalgar. Wenzel's second post, forty miles up the Fort Nelson River from the Forks, was sacked by the local Indians who slaughtered all the inhabitants and burned the fort to the ground, as was their custom. This interested me particularly, as it was a point mentioned by four different Liard Indians with whom I discussed the curious deaths in the Headless Valley region.

Understandably the fur companies shunned the Fort Nelson area for quite a while after the massacre and no further forts were built until 1865, when the Hudson's Bay Company sent a Mr Cornwallis King to protect the fur trade of the area from non-Company trappers. His fort and store were built a mile from the present Fort Nelson airport on a low mudbank. Not a very sound spot for a village. After a year nearly all the inhabitants died of scarlet fever and those who survived had their houses removed by a flood some years later: even the church had sailed away, its bell clanging drunkenly on the floodwaters.

In 1956 there were little more than a thousand inhabitants, most of whom worked either at the Canadian Air Force base or at the Alaska Highway maintenance camp — both communication links which were developed after Pearl Harbour, when the United States feared the Japanese would invade through Alaska. Now there are some three thousand inhabitants and the population doubles each winter when the forest swampland freezes and construction vehicles move in, laying new pipelines to take the abundant supplies of oil and natural gas to the power-hungry south.

The Mounties at Fort Nelson were expecting us, produced our mail, and agreed to keep a daily listening watch on their radios as soon as our boats left town. They confirmed that the river was dangerously high and would remain so for at least a week. Only the day before, the big road bridge at the southern end of the town had been crushed and swept away by a log jam.

As a further safeguard for our radio link, Ginnie and the driver of the lorry, Corporal Wallace, would set up one Racal and one Labgear radio on a hill with a rickety water-tower. At dusk each day they would listen for any messages we might send.

Steve Villars, the chief pilot and owner of Northern Air Services took us for a reconnaissance flight of the area, an experience which impressed upon me the vast scale of this untamed country. The BC–Yukon border was just a brown ribbon parting the eternal green; a double seismographic lane running south of the Petitot River. We circled a wide wind-ruffled lake which Steve said was known locally as Sandy Lake and spotted the dark specks of grazing moose along its shores. The Petitot flowed west from the lake to the Liard River entering the latter close to a blur of red and white which was Fort Liard, an Indian settlement. There were many clearings near the river: we flew lower and saw scattered moose, beaver lodges safe amid their artificial lakes, and the swirling currents of the great Liard itself emptying to the north with wide islands to confuse and stir the floodwater. To the eye, we might as well have been flying over the Amazon and the jungles of Brazil. Somewhere, lost in the northern haze, thundered the Nahanni, fed by the high glaciers of unnamed mountains. Nahanni — Indian word for 'somewhere over there and beyond'.

Fort Nelson is some eight miles from the river, but the Airport is only a mile away and here one of the charter firm managers kindly let us sleep on the floor of a disused office and prepare the equipment in one of the hangars. Once the boats were inflated, we stowed them carefully with sufficient dehydrated food for three weeks. Eighty-foot-long Terylene coils were attached to the bows of each boat and carabiner hooks fixed to all external safety lines. Long Malayan panga knives in greased sheaths were taped to the forward dodgers — easily to hand in an emergency. All perishable goods, from food and first aid equipment to film, clothing and tents, were packed in airtight plastic buckets or large blue polythene rubbish sacks, then stowed in 'mummy-bags'. These specially designed neoprene containers were lashed to the floorboards of each craft, and tailored to fit snugly beneath the spray dodgers. When fully stowed the bags were sealed with nylon lines so that, in the event

34

of a capsize, the contents should stay dry. Each boat had six separate air compartments and was designed to remain sea-worthy even if three compartments were punctured at the same time.

Richard Robinson, the BBC film director and Paul Berriff, his cameraman, were to travel in the new black RFD boat with Ben Usher, the RNLI crewman, as their helmsman. Ben was well into his thirties and a police constable serving in Bridlington, Yorkshire. In his part-time RNLI capacity, Ben had experienced many a rough sea rescue in the 16-foot RFD boats, and was sure they were the toughest inflatables on the market, but he was none too confident about the 13-foot C-Craft in which Joe Skibinski and Jack McConnell were to travel.

The third boat, the ancient silver RFD, was to be crewed by Bryn and me with Stanley Cribbett at the helm: it seemed in reason-able condition despite its age and the rough treatment it had received over the years. Whether it would stand up to the rigours of the wild rivers ahead, only time would tell.

Sleep was elusive that night on the hard floor of the hangar. Everything was ready and the floods had shown signs of abating. Local rivermen had urged us to wait a week but there was no time; we were already late in starting. Where the floodwaters had covered the land, the mud steamed and cracked, our boots sinking deep into the clinging gunk and slurping out again with effort as we manhandled the boats and bundles of kit to the river. The lorry was on firm ground some distance away and it was two hours before the loading was complete; the boats almost hidden beneath their loads. Above the mummy-bags and engine spares were lashed four-gallon jerrybags and ten-gallon barrels. Each craft carried ninety gallons of fuel as well as 1,100 pounds of equipment.

The C-Craft was alarmingly low in the water and sprang a leak as the crew fitted the 40-horse-power engine onto the transom. The boat rapidly filled with water to a depth of eight inches when the positive buoyancy of its air tubes stopped any further tendency to sink. The sun blazed down but the sky was pallid, thunderheads rimming the eastern horizon.

35

The three boats slid away from the bank, spinning in the eddies as we each tried to find somewhere to sit. Then, nudging the current, we gathered speed. A Mountie, two young Indians, and a handful of press people from Vancouver waved us off. Ginnie stood alone, looking small and forlorn in her dusty jeans. The current whipped us along and soon she was a fading image amongst the willows. For a long time the church at Old Fort Nelson was visible until the dark green line of the forest closed in behind us.

The three helmsmen tested their engines briefly before pulling the long drive-shafts clear of the water to rest on their transom hinges. We must conserve fuel wherever possible when moving with the current. Between Fort Nelson and the Arctic there is no habitation other than the Indian settlements of Fort Liard and Nahanni Butte. Neither location would necessarily have fuel available and, even if there were any, the owners might well treat it like water in the desert and not wish to sell.

The RFD boats could be steered by paddles or oars; the oars being more effective if there was room within the boat for someone to sit centrally with plenty of elbow room. We had found this impossible with all the fuel barrels in the way, and so we paddled quietly, more for steerage than motivation. We were moving at some six to seven knots and the boat's reactions to steerage proved slow and ponderous for it was low in the water and a strong under-current gripped it regardless of our paddling. So long as there was plenty of room to manœuvre away from the wicked-looking log jams, so long as each obstacle was visible to our front at least 500 yards before we reached it, we could always adjust our course sufficiently to avoid collision.

The river was 300 yards wide, both banks were thickly wooded, and the world passed by quite silently but for the rush of water past the rubber hulls, the soft plunk of paddles, and the sudden boil of converging eddies.

The other two boats moved slowly ahead and away from us. In a detached sort of way I noticed Ben's powerful barrel chest rise and fall as he pulled hard to the right: he was rowing not paddling. There was a sense of urgency about the way he tugged at his left

36

oar but his boat was quarter of a mile ahead and in clear water. Stanley and Bryn were humming softly to their paddles.

'The current's racing along just here,' Bryn mused, 'almost as though it's speeding up for a waterfall. Look at the rate we're moving past those rocks. See what I mean.'

I noticed the C-Craft crew, some three hundred yards ahead, struggling to make their way to the right. Twin splashes rose from their paddles on either side of the boat giving them the appearance of a frantic water beetle in the grip of a racing stream. Our lifejackets were lying beside the fuel drums for it was hot and we knew there were no rapids on the Fort Nelson—everyone had said so.

But there came a strange sound as of breakers lashing upon shingle; the same dull unidentifiable double boom and the rushing hiss of undertow. A feeling of indescribable apprehension accompanied this unexpected sound for, simultaneously, we were aware of a new power in the river itself. The channel ahead curved sharply right but the prevailing current sucked us to the left. The other boats were out of sight now, beyond the lie of the bend.

Great thrashing tree trunks rose and fell from the water to our left. Torn down by the force of the floods upon the elbow of the river's curve, their gnarled roots clung to the bank, the trunks trapped but moving violently to the pulse of the rushing water. We stabbed deep with the paddles, straining their wide blades through the water with our bows to the far right bank. There would be little hope for any of us once sucked into that jungle of tangled roots, through which the water drove with such force.

Sweat poured down our necks and stomachs as we fought the current, but we were losing ground. There was no time to throw away the heavy fuel which made the boat so clumsy, no time even to start the motor. A low branch whipped across Stanley's face, bringing blood. A splintered root dug into the hull tubing behind Bryn's foot and punctured it, the whole rear port compartment wrinkling slowly like a dying flower. The craft shuddered with impact against a birch trunk and spun away in rebound. Thank God the boat was rubber, not wood nor metal or we should have foundered and been drawn beneath the mass of vegetation which lined the bank.

The bend eased out and the fickle current responded to the changing camber of the riverbed by moving out to a near-central course. Bewildered by the very speed of events, we rested, breathing heavily, as the horror of the hazard so narrowly avoided was eclipsed by the scene immediately ahead. The source of the weird wind-borne rumble was an island amid the river whereon, it seemed, every log that had come with the floods was impaled. The whole force of the current, channelled by so acute a bend, ran full tilt against the upstream apex of the island and every chance piece of flotsam from floating clumps of juniper to 8o-foot logs was ensnared where the current split in two against the island.

Of the black boat there was no sign but the C-Craft was visible for a moment between the logs on the far right flank of the massive drift-pile. There was no time to notice more for the island was approaching fast and the channel to its left was a seething mass of tangled debris. We swung the nose of the old boat to the right and bent to the paddles. Stanley wrestled with the engine, swung its drive-shaft downwards until locked vertically and tugged hard at the ignition cord. With the boat angled at forty-five degrees to the direction of the current, we were gradually making headway to the right, using the classic 'ferry glide' technique which in a light-laden craft would quickly have taken us where we wished, for the current had no great bias to left or right; it simply raced pell-mell towards the log jam. For a moment I thought we would clear the island by a small margin. The motor spluttered hopefully and we rested, taking deep gulps of air. But the engine failed to start and all sound was drowned by the crash of log grinding upon log.

Stanley pulled at the starter cord again and again with hard quick jerks cursing as the fuel barrels obstructed the free pivot of his elbow. Bryn had stopped paddling and gazed over his shoulder, his knuckles white where he grasped the paddle helve.

The water was disturbed now with surging back eddies from the huge _mêlée_ of logs. Our boat ran on in the grip of the torrent which surged against and beneath the drift-pile and through a submerged forest of roots. We were some fifty yards from the island and drifting helplessly towards it. Stanley crouched over the engine, fiddling feverishly with the choke, whilst we stared up at the heaving log-pile looming ever closer with a tortured crescendo of splintering wood.

There can be little hope for us, I remember thinking: it seemed almost humorous that we should have thought of surviving some 2,000 miles on these rivers and here we were on the first day's journey with only twelve miles to our credit and succumbing to the first navigational hazard in our path.

Then it was too late to think. The boat smashed into the logs, sharp branches whipped across us and everything seemed to turn over. Someone screamed and a heavy object rammed my chest. I remember falling heavily amongst the fuel barrels; the pain of a branch ripping down my back and the shock of cold water closing over me. For a moment the boat was held by a branch and I scrabbled from the floor which was awash to the mid-tubing. The restraining branch snapped and our bows disappeared underwater, being sucked inch by inch under the churning debris. The limb of a splintered tree thudded against us and I watched mesmerised as water began to pour over the mummy-bag and the fuel drums.

A flailing branch caught Bryn and tore him loose, breaking his grip on the inner safety line. There was a frozen grin on his face as he disappeared, his outstretched hands clawing the air. The boat would soon disappear completely: we must escape onto the logs while we could. I shouted to warn Stanley and tried to scramble up onto the largest log above the boat but it was too high and too slimy to grip.

Then the craft shuddered violently. I lost my balance and fell amongst the drums, water surging over me as I lay gasping for breath. Somehow Stanley had got the engine going: throughout the chaos and the immediate hazard of drowning, he had pulled away at the starter cord, forcing himself to concentrate only on the engine. He had not even noticed Bryn disappear. He engaged gear and the 40-horse-power engine roared in reverse cavitation. There was hope.

We moved up and down and from side to side on the mummy-bag, trying to vibrate the bows free from the logs which trapped us.

A fuel drum broke loose and quite suddenly the bows rose into sight. Stanley grabbed at the tiller and the boat moved painfully backwards, steered only by our hand-over-hand pressure along the branches above and about us. Slowly but surely we fought the current through the spider's web of lashing brush. Sometimes one of us slipped or a branch broke and the motor would foul for heart-stopping moments against some unseen knot of jetsam. But now we had a chance. Despite the knowledge that Bryn must have drowned, I felt only a great surge of gratitude to little Stanley for his guts and doggedness which had saved us both. At last we broke free, shouting with relief and reversed away with care for some distance before Stanley changed gear and we moved forward; able to make a good three knots against the current.

Then I saw Bryn – or rather the faded khaki of his jacket shoulders and the black tousled mop of his hair. It seemed that some contrary underwater eddy had spewed him up further to the right where the log jam was more solid with less brush surrounding the larger trunks. His denim 'ranger' jacket had caught around a single narrow branch, its ample pockets had filled with water and, although both his arms were wrapped around the branch, each fresh surge of the current dragged his waist and legs further beneath the logs. Stemming the current with skill, Stanley backed the craft slowly towards Bryn's perch. I shouted above the din of the water and Bryn moved his head slightly. He made no effort to reply and I thought perhaps he was injured or too weak to do aught but cling to his precarious anchorage. Our bow-wave reached Bryn and added to the danger of his being dislodged, so we moved away from him and over to the side of the drift-pile to stem the current where it raced beside the logs rather than underneath them. A stout silver birch some ninety feet long was the latest arrival at the drift-pile. It jostled violently against its smaller neighbours, one of which was acting as Bryn's anchor.

We agreed on the only possible method of retrieving our absent Welshman and Stanley edged the boat carefully into position some three yards from the terminal roots of the silver birch and just to the flank of the log jam. We had both donned lifejackets and, grasping another, I jumped across to the birch, slithering on its slippery bark but gaining a hold. Edging towards Bryn on all fours, I found it necessary to hold very tight when the tree shuddered and spun in the water. It was not unlike the greasy pole event but not as enjoyable.

Coming to Bryn, I held his jacket scruff firmly whilst he donned the lifejacket, and with our combined strength, he came clear of the water. He was white, cold, and shaken but still grinning patiently. I had misjudged Bryn: his frail stature and permanently immaculate appearance concealed a tough and hardy spirit.

Whilst we were re-stacking the equipment and finding warm clothes for Bryn, the C-Craft crew had extricated themselves from an equally unpleasant situation. They too had struck the log jam but at its very edge. They had bounced off successive snags along the right-hand flank of the island where the current hugged the bank, ending up pinned between two logs. Their boat, already leaking, had filled with water, some of which had entered a fuel tank so their engine would not start until they had eventually discovered the reason and changed to the reserve tank. The BBC boat had managed to hug the right bank and their engine had started without trouble.

We had been lucky and learned our lesson about the treacherous currents of these northern rivers without tragedy. Thenceforward we ran the engines for a while each morning and started them up whenever an obstacle came in sight.

Seven miles past the log jam—which Stanley was already referring to as 'Bryn's folly'—we passed a grassy clearing on the eastern bank. This was the derelict settlement of Snake River built for the Indians in the early 1800s when the first white trappers and prospectors visited their villages. Many of the inhabitants died of smallpox or starvation and now the hamlet was reverting to forest, its brief history obliterated.

We made camp shortly before dusk. Using the machetes, we cut foliage and spread it over the deep mud. The ground by the river

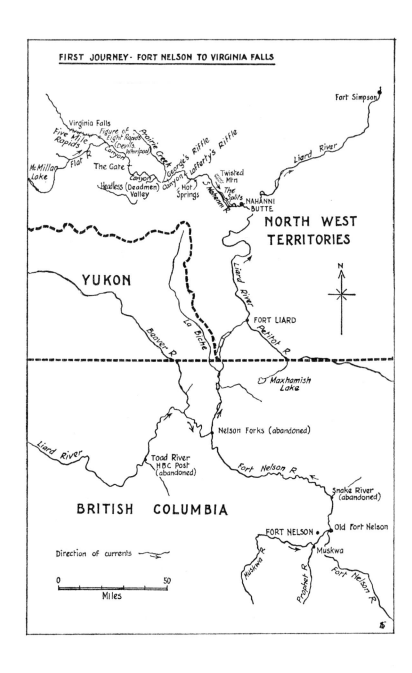

FIRST JOURNEY· FORT NELSON TO VIRGINIA FALLS

Fort Simpson

Virginia Falls
Figure of
Eight Rapids
Five Mile
Rapids
(Devils.
Whirlpool)
Prairie Creek
George's Riffle
Lafferty's Riffle
Liard River
Flat R.
Canyon
McMillan
Lake
The Gate
Canyon
Headless (Deadmen)
Valley
Canyon
Hot
Springs
Twisted
Mtn
The
Splits
S. Nahanni R.
NAHANNI
BUTTE

NORTH WEST
TERRITORIES

YUKON

Liard River

N

Beaver R.
La Biche
FORT LIARD
Petitot R.

Maxhamish
Lake

Liard River

Toad River
HBC Post
(abandoned)
Nelson Forks (abandoned)

Fort Nelson R.

Snake River
(abandoned)

BRITISH COLUMBIA

FORT NELSON
Old Fort Nelson

Muskwa R.
Muskwa
Prophet R.
Fort Nelson R.

Direction of currents

0   50
Miles

was perhaps two feet above the water level and everywhere soft and porous. The brush was dense and dripping wet but we cut away clearings for the tents and cooked dehydrated stew over hexamin blocks. The water tasted foul and no amount of teabags could prevent the feeling of gritty silt between one's teeth.

Richard, Paul, and Ben slept in two two-man tents. We had a four-man tent in which the five of us slept in a jumble of damp sleeping-bags, muddy boots and loaded pistols. The recent killing of two young girl campers in their sleeping-bags by a grizzly bear had made quite an impression on us, especially since it had occurred in a recognised park in the Rockies where grizzlies should be of a more affable disposition than their northern brethren. I found it difficult to sleep that night: there was plenty to worry about and a constant supply of mosquitoes replaced those that I managed to swat in the dark. Bryn was very talkative in his sleep but someone told him to shut up and he did so without waking.

There were thundershowers next day but the sun was a great roasting orb when the clouds left it alone. Whenever we landed with engine trouble or to wait for the others, mosquitoes and horseflies attacked with relish. From the forest came the intermittent mocking whistle of the White Crown sparrow, almost human in cadence and lilt. Canadians are convinced its song goes 'Oh, Canada, Canada, Canada', but Bryn decided that the message was 'Vive de Gaulle, Vive de Gaulle'.

The miles floated by: we swept past wicked-looking log jams, wound our way through numerous islands, and passed through a low canyon known by trappers as 'Les Roches Qui Trempent à l'Eau'.

On the evening of the second day I noticed two cut saplings planted in the mud of a narrow beach. A sharply shelving bank some twenty feet high and a narrow inlet overgrown with brush is all that Nelson Forks betrays of its presence to the river traveller. We hauled the boats onto a beach and tied the bowlines to a log.

In a month or so, all being well, we would return to this unlikely spot in need of a considerable amount of fuel to get us back up the river to Fort Nelson—105 miles away. We carried 140 gallons of fuel in drums and jerrycans up the steep bank out of reach of freak floods, and hid them in the long grass.

We camped in a rolling grassy clearing between the river and the trees. My memories of the place are coloured by the insistent attack of veritable clouds of insects, mostly mosquitoes and sandflies. 'My God,' exclaimed Bryn, spraying himself liberally with an evil-smelling aerosol, 'even a Welshman would go mad here if he were caught in the open for more than ten minutes with no repellent.' We walked around collecting wood under the mosquito nets, ate under them, chatted round the fire under them, and—most im-portant—used the Ministry of Defence lavatory paper under their protection, for Jack had already discovered to his cost that the sight of a naked white backside drove the mosquitoes quite insane with bloodlust.

Next morning the food was dehydrated, but everything was wet and muddy, and the mosquitoes, being light sleepers, awoke at the same time as we did. A fire was crackling soon after dawn, around which we sat silently like zombies for a while thawing out, and we were away from the Forks within the hour. From the left and behind us the swirling flood of the Liard pounced upon the Nelson and boiled for a while in great cartwheeling eddies, until the Nelson's green waters gave way to the livid grey of the Liard. Now we were moving at some eight knots, pulling hard at the oars and paddles to keep a central course, staring cautiously into the dull glare ahead, and awaiting only the smallest sign of a drift-pile, island, or isolated snag to lower our engines and tug them to life. If one failed to start, the crew in question would fire guns or flares to attract another craft and throw a towing line across to be pulled away from danger. So long as the boats stayed within hearing distance of one another the system worked well. We had several narrow squeaks that day and became adept with the safety lines.

We made great progress in the swift current and by evening had reached Fort Liard. Over a hundred Indians live here; some are descendants of the once proud Nahanni tribe, most are Sikannis. The only whites here serve the Indians: a saintly and enormous nurse with a surfeit of moles, a long lean Mountie with a crewcut, an eccentric French priest with a heavily pocked face and sledge-hammer hands, and a clean young Scotsman who manages the Hudson's Bay Company stores. The store was a simply constructed hut with a sign over the door saying 'HBC 1886'.

'The Company pioneers were here before anyone, except perhaps the early missionaries, and the locals say our sign stands for "Here Before Christ",' said John Miller, the Scotsman. 'Many of them resent the Company's virtual trading monopoly in the North but after all we were here long before anyone else and opened the place up. We ruled the country long before Britain established BC as a colony.'

John took us further along the bank. 'Put your tents on the grass here. It's close to the river and you can tie your boats to my mooring post. The insects are bad, but no worse than anywhere else in these parts. Anyway if you dinna like the mozzies here you might as well pack your bags and go back to the old country, because they're far worse up the Nahanni. The Indians say that Nahanni air is so thick with them that you canna starve. Just keep breathing with your mouth open and you get your daily meat ration.'

John's Canadian wife gave us moose steak, cookies and whisky. The dogs howled through the night: there are five or more to each Indian family and they work hard at the sledge traces during the long winter months, when the river is a frozen highway through the white forests.

'The best dogs sing loudest and longest when the moon comes,' John told us next day, which caused Bryn, who had slept little, to observe sourly that Fort Liard must have exceptionally high-grade hounds.

We learnt much about the area from John. There had been a Hudson's Bay Company post at Fort Liard before Fort Nelson existed. John, however, was having domestic problems. One of the few fully literate Indians in Fort Liard, a man named Dolphus, had had his skull cracked open with a metal bar the night we arrived. Although the drunken party which had resulted in this injury was apparently quite a customary occasion and quickly forgotten by all except possibly Mike the Mountie, it made life difficult for John, since good clerks were few and far between.

'Och, it's just amazing to see the way they behave,' said John. 'After a while you come to expect it. You wonder what's up wi' them if a week goes by without someone killed, shot, or knifed. And more often than not its some relation of the injured man whose done it. It's the drink: if they canna get proper hooch, they'll make do with home-made concoctions of meths or even hair-oil. Every now and again you'll find an Indian who doesna drink, but they're few and far between.'

We later met Harry Dickie, the Chief of the Fort Nelson tribe, and heard his story. It is perhaps worth recording in some detail for it is a typical case-history of many northern Indians.

Chief Harry Dickie was a Beaver Indian from Fort Vermillion. As late as the 1850s there were over four hundred Indians in the Nelson district but various 'white' epidemics reduced them by three quarters. Whilst Harry Dickie was still a young boy, his tribe lost all their horses one bad winter and he travelled north to Old Fort Nelson to work at the Hudson Bay store as 'chaw boy'. But he was strong and a skilful trapper, so he soon left for the Yukon forests where he trapped alone for marten in the winter and beaver in the spring.

By 1932 he was doing well and after two good seasons he filled his canoe with thirty-nine bales of high-grade furs and paddled to Nelson once the river had dropped. Two gunmen stole all his furs before he could sell them and escaped down the Liard by boat. The Mounties eventually found the furs and arrested the thieves on the US border. Harry added with disgust, 'They spent three years in jail but as soon as they were released they came back to the Liard and carried on trapping!'

Harry had then married an Indian girl from the now derelict hamlet of François, south of Fort Liard; the marriage taking place at Nelson Forks. After three years Bella, his wife, had died of tuberculosis like so many people in the forties. Many too died of pneumonia for there was no medicine and no way of getting the sick to a hospital. In 1942 a 'flu epidemic swept through the land, killing off most of the children and old people. The rivers too were high that year and many of the hunters were drowned. There was no communication with the outside world except a small weather station at Nelson Forks but that burned down one night and then there was nothing.

Harry and the Indians then began to lose heart for the Second World War came to an end, Fort Nelson began to flourish and many white men arrived who ruined the trapping. In Harry's own words:

In the old days we had always respected the Game Warden. We called him Ah-Tee-Ah-Tee, 'the man that tells the truth', and his word was law. Then the great war ended and many white men came to Nelson country to trap. Before that each Indian had two traplines which he would work one after the other. But then the Warden gave one of the two from each of us to the white men. This is still so. Look at our reserve here at 295: we are surrounded by traplines owned by the white men. They have all the beaver lines along the river banks in front of our lines, so they get nearly all the beaver pelts.

The situation is bad. Our people can't get good jobs in Nelson as they have no education to compare with the white man's, although they get free local schooling and can be sent to Federal boarding schools when they reach their teens. They get into trouble because they go on welfare and drink away their money, so the children are hungry and learn bad ways. The whites have regular jobs so they only trap at weekends and on holidays. Most of them don't know how to skin and stretch the furs so they bring them to our women for this work. Here again they take advantage of us for we are in no position to bargain. They give our women only a dollar a skin which is the same wage as twenty-five years ago.

For a long while after his early trapping days in the Yukon, Harry had worked as a pilot on the Hudson's Bay Company river barges between Fort Nelson and Fort Simpson. Then a school was built in Nelson and he became janitor there for nine years. Otherwise, without the regular pay, he might well have starved, for his trapline was dogged by bad luck: twice it was destroyed by forest fires and then all his food caches were stolen.

Once Harry had settled to a regular job, he remarried, and now has four boys and seven girls. Soon known and respected as the fairest and most reliable Indian at Fort Nelson, he was elected as Chief by the tribe with the approval of the Indian Affairs Department. For eighteen years before Harry, the Chief had been one George Behn whose mother was a Sikanni and father a German trapper—they had never married. George had proved a youthful miscreant, to put it lightly, and was sent to a reform school. In this way he had received some education and learnt English, unlike most of the other Indians at the time. So when the Alaska Highway came to Nelson, George was elected as Chief since—despite his criminal record—he could speak English and therefore act as liaison man between the Indians and the various white institutions. But leopards seldom change their spots and corruption was soon rife. Everyone was much relieved when Harry became Chief.

*   *   *

'The English were always very mad, no? I, who know the rivers like the back of my hand, can tell you—you will never reach the waterfall in these rubber tubs of yours. When the water is bad and the waves are so big, then maybe it is good to have such rafts. But to fight up against the power of the great Nahanni. In no way. I tell you, you must use a boat like mine with a flat bottom, and thirty feet long. Then maybe you make it. Otherwise you get nowhere at all.'

Father Mary jumped up from his tatty leather chair and fiddled about with the innards of the old wood-burning stove. He muttered away all the while. If one listened intently and managed to hear the little priest's garbled soliloquy above the clatter of the coffee pot and the hysterical dogs outside, one found oneself being harangued simultaneously in a mixture of French and *incroyable* Maurice Chevalier English, with every now and again an unintelligible Indian expletive thrown in for good measure.

The Father was preparing a supper of moose meat, cookies and

In the labyrinth of the Splits, trappers and Indians have died of starvation, crazed by the teeming insects.

The site of the original cabin of the McLeods at the time of their murder and decapitation

Climbing to inspect the Devil's Whirlpool where the German Expedition were all drowned

thick cauldrony coffee. He patted Stanley cheerfully on the back, so that he spilled his coffee, and shook an emphatic carrot at us as he continued.

'I tell you—and I have been in this place for fifteen long years—you must borrow an Indian riverboat. Only then can you hope to reach the great waterfall.'

Before it got too hot, he removed a finger with which he had been stirring the stew and licked it appreciatively.

'I am a cook *sans pareil*,' he observed, 'with great talent, as you will agree when you have tasted this *magnifique* stew. The moose will taste like lamb.' Culinary credentials disposed of, he returned to our problems.

'From here to the Nahanni is simple, but you must be careful for the water is high and dangerous. Then you have maybe one hundred and forty miles of bad fast river. It is from the glaciers, very cold. Those men who disappeared up the Nahanni, they were no fools, you know. They were all men who knew the bush well, but in that country one mistake is too many. One mistake and—whoosh, it is too late. There will be many dangers before you reach the Flat River—where the gold is found and where they discover the skeleton of Jorgensen *sans tête*, but remember, the worse water lies beyond the Flat, where the Germans were drowned in 1963. Only one of their bodies floated down and was found. The others, they must have been sucked down into the Devil's Whirlpool.'

Father Mary doled out helpings of moose stew with an outsize ladle and began to tuck into his own portion with relish. With equal relish he continued his catalogue of hazards.

'From the Flat to the Falls is the most *difficile* region, for the water races down like a galloping horse. I have seen it myself: it is *incroyable*. No Indians live up the Nahanni, no people at all. But there is always this feeling that someone is watching. One winter I am in Nahanni country with my dogs. I have size eleven overshoes, you understand, which make a very big print in the snow. But I come to the prints of a grizzly and I tell you I am glad to meet only the prints and not the bear herself, for her paw prints were even bigger than my own track.'

D   49

Father Mary's house was a shambling two-storey place with bare boards and a friendly clutter of bric-à-brac in every corner, on every peeling wall. Upstairs a long low room served as a repair shop for outboard engines, obviously neglected and maltreated by their Indian owners and brought to the Father to tinker with. A novel way, I reflected, of reaching the souls of his flock.

Two of our own outboards had been running badly and, the following day, the Father came to our boats and adjusted the Evinrudes in some way—much to Stanley's ire and indignation. For several weeks thereafter every flutter in the engines' beat, a mere hint of obstinacy in their response to the starter cords, brought a stream of invective from Chief Engineer Stanley which must have made Father Mary's ears burn.

We bade our new friends farewell and left Fort Liard on the swollen waters that lead to the Arctic. The Flutch and the Flett Rapids lay dormant, only rippling the veneer of floodwater into a gentle swell above their hidden teeth. Flotillas of islets, lurking creeks and snyes, tangled clumps of willow wherein woodpeckers — as big and bouncy as cockerels—chackered their anger at our passing. In widening loops the Liard split the swampy forest for a hundred miles. From a low irregularity on the northern horizon, beyond the broken summits of the Liard range, a mountain of singular shape rose hourly larger and more striking before us. We followed the river's snaking course to the east and west, but always swung back to the great bell-shaped ridge that dominated the landscape.

In the hour before dusk the forest was quiet and the mountain reared close above us. In the fastness of its shadow we left the Liard where it flowed to the east to join the wide Mackenzie on its way to the Arctic. A narrow backwater, easing through islands of swamp-grass, led us to another channel where the water ran green and powerful from the west. The boats nosed into the current; motors running poorly and progress slow. But a new excitement stirred us for this was the Nahanni, the dangerous river.

3

The Twisted Mountain

THE NAHANNI RISES IN THE LOFTY SELWYN MOUNTAINS, DRAINING
an area of 14,300 square miles and flowing south-east through the
North West Territories to join the Liard at Nahanni Butte. At first
it is turbulent as it rushes through the granite ranges of the Funeral
and Tlogotsho Mountains, then it quietens down for 200 miles until
it cascades over the Virginia Falls, 316 feet of sheer buttress. The
river then drops well over a thousand feet between the Falls and
Nahanni Butte, where we were, so that, even where there are no
rapids, it is moving at over ten knots and considerably more in
narrow gorges where the current bottlenecks or splits around
islands. Remembering how painfully we had struggled up the
Thames against a five-knot tide race, and then with only 1,000
pounds of simulated cargo, I wondered how we would cope against
the millrace of the Nahanni.

The whole Nahanni area is remote and until recently few people
have been there. For centuries the Nahanni Indians were the
exclusive hunters and traders of their river, keeping other tribes and
early white pioneers away from their land with threats and fearful
legends. They killed many of the Mackenzie River Indians during their annual fishing migration to the north-east, and the
southern Slave Indians still refuse to travel in the Tlogotsho,
believing the remnants of the Nahanni tribe to inhabit these
distant peaks. No factual history of the Nahannis is known before

the turn of the century, although a few pioneers and Klondike gold-seekers are said to have gone up the river before then. None of them ever emerged again, so their tales were never told. Then in 1906 Poole Field, an ex-policeman, befriended the Nahannis and set up a fur-trading cabin at Nahanni Butte. Word spread south that these Indians were not as fierce as earlier reports had made out: soon a questing force of migratory prospectors was hovering at Fort Simpson, eastern gateway to the area. One of them, Murdoch McLeod of the Hudson's Bay Company, made friends with a Nahanni who divulged the location of an Indian gold mine along the Flat River tributary. McLeod collected sledges and equipment, then, with his two brothers, made a hazardous overland journey from the Stikine to the Flat River. They found gold and returned to Fort Liard in a boat made of sluice boxes.

Gold greed was strong and a few years later, two of the brothers returned with a third man, a Scottish engineer who in Mountie reports is variously called Wilkerson, Green or Weir. The men were never seen alive again and, in 1909, another two McLeod brothers (they seem to have been a prolific clan) led a search party some ninety miles up the Nahanni to a wide valley where two skeletons were found. The skulls were missing and the clothing on the bodies had been burnt.

Many people accused the Nahanni Indians of the murder but others pointed out that the third man, Weir, was missing. Fortunately for the latter's posthumous reputation, whatever his actual name, a third skeleton, also lacking a skull, was found by Indians some distance away. Very soon the valley where the skeletons were found came to be known as Deadmen Valley, now its official title.

The mountain range enclosing the valley was called the Headless Range and the whole South Nahanni Valley was labelled the Headless Valley or the Valley of the Vanishing Men by the Canadian press. In the 1930s most of the Nahanni tribes were decimated by smallpox epidemics; their legends dying with them. Then during the sixty years between the McLeod brothers' sensational deaths and our own arrival, some thirty men, mostly prospectors, had died or disappeared in the Valley. This is quite a fair number when you consider the very small number of annual travellers to the region, all of whom were tough characters considered well able to look after themselves.

Two teams had unsuccessfully tried to reach the Virginia Falls by boat in the 1960s, one with tragic consequences, and eight different expeditions had set out in 1970 but all had turned back before reaching the Falls except for a Mr Mikes who, when his own craft failed, borrowed an Indian scow from Nahanni Butte and managed to reach the waterfall after many difficulties. One man had made repeated attempts and had become something of an authority on river travel in British Columbia; he was John Ferries, a Vancouver doctor. He and I had been in correspondence and he had given me much good advice. He had travelled in everything from canoes to long riverboats, the traditional flat-bottomed scows of the north. In 1968 he had bought a 16-foot inflatable boat, not unlike our own, and powered by a 35-horse-power motor (which has virtually the same performance as a 40-horse-power one). After numerous attempts at lightening his cargo, hugging backwaters, and pulling the boat through shallows, Dr Ferries and his crew had to admit defeat: the current was too strong and the journey too long. But he had determined to try again and built a 30-foot scow, specially designed for the Nahanni and powered by two 50-horse-power motors. He was planning to leave Fort Nelson a month after us when the rivers were lower and the currents less powerful. We were not to know it then but Dr Ferries was again to be frustrated by the Nahanni's narrow canyons and unrelenting power.

With inflatable boats our main problem would be getting our craft to plane or glide. They must be able to reach the speed where their bows would lift clear of the water so that water displacement and friction would be minimal and maximum cruising speed could be held without full throttle. This is not possible with a cargo that exceeds a set maximum weight and our fuel requirements for the journey to the Falls constituted anything but a light load. Seventy-five gallons would be required for each boat; meaning 750 pounds on board without any equipment or crew.

Doctor Ferries was adamant that a 16-foot inflatable driven by a 35- or 40-horse-power motor with a normal (11 × 9 inches) working propeller would plane at thirteen knots through slack water only if the total cargo weight was under 1,200 pounds and this included the 150-pound engine. With anything more than this critical weight factor, the boat would not plane and would become a displacement craft, dragging heavily through the water and feeling the full effect of any adverse current.

On the Nahanni there would be the added unfavourable factor of slippage or cavitation of the propeller when moving against the strong surging currents which would greatly reduce the efficiency of the motors. Furthermore it is a silt river with continually moving sandbanks in which submerged roots are ensnared. It was apparent that we must move at all times with the motors at maximum thrust if we were to progress at all, therefore considerable damage could occur to the propellers if they struck a submerged snag, invisible in the ever muddy water.

Once a propeller loses its original aerodynamic shaping through distortion it becomes far less effective. Although they added considerably to our weight problem, I had brought eighteen propellers with us since they were by all accounts the most vulnerable and vital factor in the whole business of planing.

To give us a chance of success on the Nahanni we needed an Indian riverboat in which to put the 300 gallons of fuel needed to take us the 150 miles to the Falls. In Fort Nelson and Fort Liard the riverboats had been too large and too expensive but, soon after arriving at Nahanni Butte, an Indian named Baptiste Matoux approached us. He spoke excellent English and agreed to hire us his old riverboat for fifty dollars and a sample of our Black and White whisky. The boat was a 32-footer, flat-bottomed and fashioned after the manner of an English punt. The bow end was covered with planking which provided a useful sprayproof nook for storage, and a rounded Sampson post stood proud from the bow decking for the attachment of a mooring rope.

After consideration of the fuel problem, we deflated the BBC boat and transferred their equipment to our new acquisition.

It was as well that we gave the riverboat a loaded test run for the engine, an old 35-horse-power one, overheated and gave up the ghost. Stanley declared its water-pump defective and we returned it to Baptiste whose eyebrows rose high in elaborate surprise at his motor's uselessness. He was a wiry young man who effected the cowboy style popular amongst most Canadian Indians: skintight blue jeans, black Stetson, neckerchief, and high-heeled leather boots.

We spent the night in a bunkhouse cabin belonging to the local trapper's son and, soon after dusk, were visited by Baptiste and a podgy friend of his whom he introduced as Sambo. Both were extremely drunk.

As they entered Baptiste saw Ben Usher sitting on the floor. He stopped, becoming quite rigid and stared fixedly at our policeman with an expression of almost venomous hate. The atmosphere became electric in the silence, until Bryn approached Baptiste and introduced himself. The Indian seemed to relax and soon forgot about Ben: he wanted more whisky and wouldn't listen when I assured him that our two remaining bottles were strictly for medicinal purposes. For an hour they sat with us, often shouting at one another in anger, and leaving only after our promise to visit Baptiste's house the next day to buy moccasins from his wife. When sober, Baptiste was a charming and most intelligent man.

We rose early for the mosquitoes were bad despite our green coils of slow-burning repellent which smoked throughout the night.

There was a government schoolteachers' house which was vacant, but not locked up. I went inside with Stanley who attacked the panel of knobs and dials on a radio-phone in the sitting room. Soon the room was buzzing with the crackle of static and mush as Stan twiddled the tuning handle. An operator at Watson Lake replied who would relay our message to Ginnie at Fort Nelson.

We needed a second 40-horse-power engine for the riverboat for it responded only sluggishly to a single engine, and a spare cylinder head for one of the Evinrudes which had a faulty plug thread. Also a supply of a more effective mosquito repellent.

Ours was the 1948 War Office issue which had doubtlessly proved murderously efficient against the Malayan communist mosquitoes, but had lost its potency over the years. Jack McConnell had even complained that he suffered worse attacks after applying his repellent than before; suggesting that the 'wee brutes' actually liked the stuff.

We met a dark-haired, keen-eyed man named Brian Doke, the brother-in-law of Don Turner, the local big-game hunter. He was living in Don's cabin at the time and invited us in. He seemed to hate the plague of insects as much as we did, spraying the room carefully as soon as we were through the mesh door—accompanied by a cloud of bugs.

'It's only the females that suck your blood,' he said, 'so's their eggs can feed. After they hatch, the mums lay down and die.' Brian was a bush guide. He knew the country well and respected it.

He told us of a moose-hunter who capsized only twelve miles from Nahanni Butte, lost all his kit and twisted an ankle. They found him nine days later half-starved and demented by the insects.

Another hunter in Nahanni country had been followed for quarter of a mile by a black bear. He must have turned round and seen the bear a fraction too late for his half-eaten body was found close to his loaded rifle. His skull however was comfortingly intact. A helicopter-pilot later came to search for the killer bear and, spotting it too close for comfort, stepped back into the revolving heliblade which scalped him neatly.

Brian's cabin thermometer showed it to be eighty-six degrees Fahrenheit in the shade although it was only nine o'clock in the morning. We walked through the bush wearing mosquito veils and gloves, and our necks itched from running sweat.

In the clearing some thirty small log cabins housed the Indians. Snow-shoes and small outboard motors hung from nails. Battered dog-sleighs lay propped in the shade of alder clumps. Old men and children sat around watching us silently, hands in pockets. A white one-eyed dog howled long and wild. Like two hundred other dogs around the clearing it was chained to a stake and had dug a hole to hide in from the leaden heat and the mosquitoes.

I saw the wrinkled face of a man shift its expression into a vile grin, a sort of rippling death mask. Then he moved and the sun's rays glinted on the moving wings of a hundred writhing feasting insects. Only his tired old eyes were free of them.

By his feet a child picked wild strawberries, flapping its hand at the mosquitoes every now and again. In a few years perhaps it would give up the unequal struggle and would flap no more.

No plane had come with our spares so we spent the next day climbing the Butte. We crossed the river at dawn and reached the lower end of the towering escarpment before the heat grew oppressive. A gap had already grown between the soldiers and the others. I waited with Jack and Joe: Stanley had stayed below to work on the engines.

Bryn was clearly tiring and none too pleased with life.

'Look here Ran, if you clear off into the distance with the only rifle, and we bump into a bear, our pistols won't be much help. Don't forget you lot are fit whilst we've been sitting around in offices for months.'

Ben growled his assent looking as dour and grim under his wide-brimmed Stetson as John Wayne facing a lynch-mob.

Richard and Paul moved around us filming. They were sweating freely and were unable to wear mosquito nets whilst they filmed. Obviously a dedicated team.

But the heat grew intense and the insects were maddening; infinitely worse if one stopped or slowed down. For six hours we stumbled upwards through thick bush, forcing a way through the thorn and deep undergrowth. The mountain was 5,000 feet high with a magnificent view in every direction. We moved slowly but surely upwards and reached the summit not long after noon. The water-bottles were empty and great was our delight when Joe spotted a spring only 200 feet below us. The water was ice-cool and delicious. There were less insects at this height and a faint breeze helped keep them away.

An eagle soared along the cliff top, jinking away only fifty feet from the summit ridge where we sat, legs dangling over a sheer void of 3,000 feet. It was the largest bird I had seen, greater even than the golden eagles of Skye.

To the west, the Nahanni shimmered away in a series of wide

oxbow loops with high forested banks. Then, in the middle distance, the land lay low about the river which, with no banks to contain its main stream split out at random into a vast network of shallows, called the Splits. Through binoculars, I tried to plot and memorise a potential route through this veritable maze of netherland. I soon gave up for a myriad minor channels confused and sidetracked the eye. Some, it seemed, meandered for many miles only to shelve away into cul-de-sacs.

Many travellers, intent on finding the long-lost gold of the Upper Nahanni were lost for ever in these Splits and it was easy to see why.

For the return journey we divided, Joe accompanying the others. Jack and I—hoping to reach the river quickly and attract the attention of Stanley on the far bank by pre-arranged gunfire— descended a steep gully to the east of the Butte where, from above, the going looked better than our ascent route.

We slid down for 2,000 feet amidst a shower of rocks and rotten tree trunks. I lost my water-bottle and shared Jack's which we soon finished, for there was no breeze below the summit ridge and the heat was stifling.

Jack missed his footing as we slithered from ledge to ledge. He cartwheeled through the air and smashed into a tangle of juniper. The wood was decayed and snapped off under his weight. He came to rest against a firm boulder some fifty yards down the slope: his shirt was torn and his face and arms bruised and scratched. The radio pack had protected his back and no limbs were broken. We continued slowly, wanting water and cursing aloud at the insects.

The slope eased then and the bush closed about us. From the dry foliage countless mosquitoes hummed and settled on us. Jack slapped my shoulder above the rucksack and showed me his hand, bright red with my blood from the squashed mosquitoes.

It required much effort to force a way through the thorn and alder climbing over charred tree trunks, and our eyes stung from the running sweat mixed with repellent.

Every few hundred yards we collapsed through exhaustion and the heat. I remember thinking it extremely strange since we were both fit. Both the river and the mountain were invisible. There was only the dense brush on every side and the moving halo of insects with their frenetic ululating whine.

It was an effort even to undo the compass pouch, so I left it dangling from its neck lanyard. Later it was wrenched away unseen by a branch as I lurched through the undergrowth. We followed the sun then, heading south-west where the river lay.

I don't remember ever having felt so utterly worn out. One thing in particular revealed the low ebb of morale I had reached. In the Special Air Service, a man would be thrown out of the regiment if he were ever seen dragging his rifle along the ground, no matter how tired he might be. In this Nahanni bush, I gave in to the miasma of fatigue, and let the loaded rifle trail behind, held limply by its barrel.

Only by keeping moving in the thicker bush could we stay relatively free from the maddening attention of the insects. The second we collapsed they were upon us in their thousands, attracted by the smell of sweat and the blood from their squashed predecessors which dripped from our arms and necks. We said nothing for our throats were dry and feathery from swallowing the insects.

A crackling of breaking alder sounded ahead and the ground trembled as some great beast moved away. Soon afterwards we broke through into a depression of muskeg with small foetid pools of rust-coloured water. We flung ourselves on the oozing moss and drank deep. I don't remember any particular taste to the water, but the swamp stank and we left after filling the water-bottle, moving with renewed strength and unable to explain to each other our previous pathetic behaviour. An hour later we struck a well-used game trail and followed it to the river. Jack fired a couple of shots to bring Stanley over in a boat and I left him drinking from the river. There was a wide trail running beside the water which must lead to the Turners' cabin, the only one on the north bank. Brian Doke, their son-in-law, had told us about it. Swatting wildly at the insects I moved off down the trail but soon noticed Jack's absence. Growing worried, I returned to the bank and, on approaching it, heard Jack crying my name. I broke into a run and found him where he had been drinking. He had sunk into the mud to his thighs. His struggles had only caused him to sink further and his face was black with mud where he had frantically swept at the eager cloud of mosquitoes. With some climbing rope and the aid of a nearby tree Jack was soon free. One of his eyelids had swollen so that the eye was hidden and his face and arms were puffed out like a Michelin man.

There was no sound of an outboard engine so we continued to the Turners. Mrs Turner was alone in the cabin and welcomed us despite our muddy boots and indelicate aroma.

She was a little woman in her late fifties wearing glasses and baggy trousers. Her long dark hair fell free about narrow shoulders. Tea, orange, and cookies soon appeared on the kitchen table. Around us the great varnished logs gleamed in the dim light between wolf and bear skins and fine landscape paintings.

She had a small lonely face. It could be no place for a woman by herself, especially in the long bitter winters. Her four children were grown up and absent and Dick, her husband, spent much of his time upriver trapping and prospecting. She could never be certain he would return: too many experienced men had disappeared in the bush.

'I've been here thirty-eight years,' she said, spraying repellent on the mesh door, 'and I'm still not used to them. This place would be a paradise in summer but for the insects and, believe me, they're far worse after a mild winter. Experienced trappers have been found bushed and out of their minds after a few hours lost in the mosquito bush.'

Surprisingly Mrs Turner had come from Halifax in Yorkshire when only seventeen and had lived in a variety of home-made log cabins in the far north ever since.

'We opened a little trading store here for the Indians,' she told us, stroking a large black Alsatian that lay beside her, 'but had to close it a year back because of freight charges. Dick used to run his own stores barge from Nelson but even then we had to add quite a bit to cover our freight costs. A Coca-Cola costing fifteen cents in Nelson would be fifty cents here. The Indians complained and eventually we had to close down. Now they've opened a government store across the river. God knows how it survives if indeed it does.'

The black Alsatian was licking its chest tenderly. Mrs Turner showed us where she had removed a porcupine quill that morning.

'They never learn, he'll be in pain for days because of the quills but the very next time he sees a porky, he'll be right after it hammer and tongs. You have to remove the quills with great care or they break off and work themselves into the flesh. The Indians use the quills for their bead work, you know. They beat them flat, dye them and use them for embroidery. Look at these moccasins and the larger mukluks, how fine their workmanship is. But they seldom produce this quality nowadays.'

The sound of an outboard engine came to us, so we thanked Mrs Turner and left. The others were waiting along the bank and Stanley ferried the seven of us across to our bunkhouse.

Perhaps it was the exertions of the day which strained nerves; Joe was despondent and told me he had been sorely tempted to carry on down the mountain without the others. They had refused to see the good sense of keeping a reasonable pace going and had had long halts despite the insects. Richard too cornered me in the bunkhouse, wanting a number of assurances, especially a definite date for our arrival in Vancouver.

I reiterated my intention to reach the American border by mid-October but pointed out that one could not be adamant about this since there was no way of telling what unforeseen mishaps and obstacles we might meet *en route*. But Richard would settle for nothing less than a firm date. He and Paul had won an international award for their film of the Grand Canyon kayak expedition the year before and I felt they were now judging things by the standards of this other trip. Superficially such a comparison seemed reasonable, for both journeys involved wild North American rivers and in each case the film team recorded events from a powered inflatable.

But here any similarity ended. Their journey was a straightforward descent by a dozen kayaks and two 30-foot inflatables down a portion of the Colorado River which, though dangerous, is annually descended by some eight thousand tourists. The expedition was mounted by a university team who had navigated the route twice before, and since the journey only took ten days it was possible to eat in grand style: T-bone steaks and milk are fine when cargo weight problems are minimal. With our boats' critical planing problem, we had to make do with lightweight dehydrated army rations.

Sometimes it is undoubtedly best for an expedition leader to lay down the law and stick to it, although it may lead to muttering amongst the ranks. But so long as it does not endanger life or the aims of the expedition a middle course of diplomatic appeasement is more useful.

* * *

The airstrip at Nahanni Butte is a widened extension of the village firebreak. A Beaver from Northern Air Services arrived late on July 13th with our supplies—an ancient 35-horse-power engine and an Evinrude cylinder head. Stanley worked on the engines by torchlight whilst I sat behind him beating him over the head and back with a rolled-up map to discourage the bugs.

Three hundred gallons of petrol had to be mixed with oil at the correct ratio and transferred into ten-gallon drums or neoprene bags. One of the 45-gallon drums was from the little government store at the Butte and we found it to contain one third water and two thirds petrol. The storeman was unrepentant and said it was the suppliers' fault, not his.

If a mere droplet of water reached the petrol intake of a motor, it would stop and quite possibly lead to a capsize. Brian Doke told us that many riverboat pilots had been drowned through using watered-down petrol and aeroplane bush pilots had crashed because of similarly treated Avgas fuel.

Father Mary had also warned us of this danger and given us his black floppy felt hat.

'Always filter your gas through my hat,' he said gravely, 'or you will regret it. First wet the hat well in the river, then pour away.

You will be surprised how much water remain in my hat when the gas go through.'

Next morning the riverboat was half full of water and threatening to sink. We bailed out the water and found a leak in the rear transom which, on closer inspection, appeared to be cracked and rotten: alarming—since the full strain of two 40-horse-power outboards must be taken by the transom alone.

Some amateur caulking with Bostik fixed the leaks and we left hurriedly; before something else conspired to hold us up at that godforsaken hamlet.

Ten miles of wide rolling loops ceased abruptly past the second island, for here the low banks narrowed and threshers all but barred the channel. As though motivated from below, these fallen giants rose and fell like isolated fangs, water cascading from their branches as they rose clear of the water; a resounding splash as they plunged under the surface again.

Bryn tensed on first sighting the menacing threshers. He seized his binoculars and, balancing on the laden mummy-bag up front, scrutinised the river ahead.

'There's a channel to the left,' he shouted. 'We'll never make it through those things. Go left or we'll be hit.'

But the left-hand channel was merely a shallow snye and Stanley nosed the boat skilfully through the threshers themselves, scraping the rubber sometimes when the current washed us sideways against the plunging logs but always finding a route without endangering the boat. There was a dull roaring noise in that area as the water sucked through a forest of submerged roots.

The little C-Craft followed us with ease, darting in between the obstacles like a water-beetle, but the riverboat had its length to think about and Ben must have had some unpleasant moments jerking his two tillers from side to side to counter the waltzing current.

Then the threshers were behind us but for the isolated few which stud the whole river indicating sandbars.

The scenery had changed: the banks fell away on either side like the widening neck of a funnel. Now the water made a different sound, the low grinding roar of gravel silt sucked hither and thither by the rushing shallows. We were moving extremely slowly, against the surging water of a vast flood plain strewn with sandbars, wooded shingle islands, huge drift-piles, and queer dead-looking forests of snags where uprooted trees lodged in the riverbed until torn away by the torrent and caught against the next downstream snare.

'No place for rubber boats,' muttered Stanley, shielding his eyes against the reflected glare, 'if the engine seizes anywhere here, we won't stand a chance in hell. Look at the way the current races past those islands.'

But the engines gave no trouble and the boats struggled further into the maze. The water was icy despite the great heat: we wore nothing but shorts—except Bryn who remained correctly attired—and by noon our shoulders were red and uncomfortable. It was wonderful to be free of insects: so long as we kept moving only the large horseflies visited us and they were easy targets for a paddle.

The map showed a wide variety of channels which at first seemed to agree with the various forks, T-junctions, and double bends that we came to.

The blue-grey ridge of the Twisted Mountain peeped over the western horizon and I thought of Father Mary's warning:

'The Nahanni is captured by three great canyons. When the weather is terrible to the north in the mountains of its birth, the sun is maybe shining to the south of the canyons. Therefore you have no warning, maybe you are camping on a low beach in the Splits and, *voilà*, the water is roaring over the flood plain. She can rise sixty feet within the canyons and that is much water. To avoid this, you must camp by the Twisted Mountain. There you find high ground for sure.'

The hours wore on, and conditions deteriorated. Obviously I had lost the main channel—if indeed there was one. Nothing agreed with the map now and anyway there was no time to study it. Perched at the very front of each boat, one man speared the water every few yards with a cut sapling; slender enough to slip in and out of the water without too much strain on the wrist, yet sufficiently robust not to snap in the current.

Each time my stick struck the riverbed and I shouted, Stanley swung across the river and probed upstream until we found a deep enough channel. Often there was none and the propeller struck rock giving us a choice to jump overboard and tug the boat upstream of the shallows or, if our route looked hopeless, turn about and go back until we found an alternative channel.

It was disturbing that the ground was so low and swampy: the whole alluvial plain was at any time liable to sudden inundation and there was no dependable place of refuge. One could not even be sure of finding a way out again should it prove impossible to break through the Splits.

As time went by the Twisted Mountain, though easily visible now, remained far to our north. I searched eagerly for some high ground where we might safely spend the night, but many of the islands were mainly driftwood and in constant danger of disintegration by the river.

Regardless of which might be the wider channel, I followed the right-hand fork whenever possible. This led to much pushing and pulling and halts whilst Stanley replaced chewed-up propellers. All the while the looming rim of the Twisted Mountain grew tall and black above the swamp forest to our right. A solid oasis, it seemed to me, in all this mad rushing plain, where water played with and destroyed everything of substance; building great islands one day to tear them down the next.

Shortly before dusk we broke through a belt of flattened alder, tangled with the residual scum of many floods, and reached the base of the towering cliffs. The mountain bounded the northern flank of the flood plain and put us back at an identifiable spot on the map. The bank sloped quite steeply to a sandy shelf occupied by low patches of willow and spruce. A high wind howled along the cliffs, sucking upwards in gyrating thermals and snaking outwards with violent gusts that whipped up sand and leaves, stinging our eyes when we landed. The riverboat chugged in beside us as we unloaded the tents and supplies.

Distant gunshots came from the south as I carried the cooking pots up the bank, shielding my eyes from the flying sand. Visibility was low but I saw Stanley push the silver boat from the beach, jump into it and pull at the starter cord. After a long while the sound of labouring engines came through the yellow gloom. Stanley had found the C-Craft in trouble, its engine's clutch gone and losing ground with hardly enough power for steerage. Somehow he had caught their line whilst keeping his own boat away from the sandbars and had towed the lame C-Craft, making headway against the current only because his own boat was virtually empty of equipment.

We camped in the bushes, for our tent pegs were torn from the sand by the gale. After the guy-ropes were secured to saplings instead, the tents remained stable and we ate inside them listening to the wild chant of the wind around the cliff face. A thunderstorm broke and lashed the tents: we lay within munching stew, except for Stanley who worked with his torch beneath a groundsheet, replacing the defective clutchplate. The thunder rolled and crackled around spitting tongues of lightning and everywhere rivulets clawed down through sand and rock to the Nahanni and the water rose to cover many of the sandbars and islands where we must surely have camped had we not reached the Twisted Mountain.

4

The Valley of Vanishing Men

A CRASHING ABOUT IN THE BUSH AWOKE ME. WHATEVER IT WAS
snapped a guy-rope so that a very wet bit of tent enveloped my face.
I felt for my torch and pistol, having visions of a great furry thing
with slavering chops.

My stomach fluttered wildly when the mosquito netting parted
and the torch beam lit up a face far more horrible than a grizzly's.

A large black nose surrounded by matted hair was set off by
bloodshot eyes with tiny pupils. Its skin was blotched with black
smudges and smears of yellow grease. Its mouth hung open in
surprise at the sudden light. It seemed to have emerged from the
river since water streamed from its hairy chin in rivulets.

The apparition peered around the entrance flap and swore in a
Devon accent. 'Thank Gawd that's finished. I thought I'd never
get the bloody nuts off. The rain just about washed me away. The
river's up a couple of feet and still rising.' Stanley wiped his nose
on the dripping cuff of his anorak, further dispersing the grime.
'And where do those Scotsmen think the workers are going to get
some sleep then, eh?'

Stan stripped naked outside whilst I tried to make some space for
his sleeping-bag between Bryn and me.

By placing my feet within the sleeping-bag against Bryn's rear end
and pushing firmly, both he and the two Scotsmen concertina'd
leaving an eighteen-inch gap for Stanley who, wringing wet, leapt
into the space before the other three puffed out again.

The monotonous and irritating duet of Bryn's snoring and Stanley's chattering teeth kept me awake for a while, and a desire to visit the bushes grew stronger, finally becoming irresistible. There being only one entrance, it was necessary to tread on at least two bodies on the way out. I chose Bryn, since a foot on his back might distract his adenoids, and Joe, because he changed from animal to mineral for a regulation eight hours after falling asleep and was nigh impossible to wake before the eight hours were up.

Outside the rainclouds were gone and the night was balmy with an iridescent luminosity which flickered in weird animation along the ramparts of the Twisted Mountain. After the regularity of the cliffs elsewhere, these huge contorted slabs were grotesque evidence of nature's violence.

* * *

All the next morning we struggled through shallow rapids where powerful eddies swept beneath fallen deadwood. There were no high waves nor whirlpools to worry about yet, only the propeller-buckling shallows and the jagged snares awaiting us should an engine fail.

The riverbed was not always gravel. Once the Indian riverboat became firmly jammed on a silt bank and all three crews had to heave at its bowline for an hour before we could move on. The current would grip the boat as soon as we managed to free it and pull the lot of us through the icy water back down to the last shallow before Ben could start the engines. Struggling against the flow impeded our progress. In between the sandbanks were areas of soft black mud into which we sank and from which much effort was needed to 'un-glug' our legs. Fortunately the weather held and we came through the Splits by late afternoon.

Lunch was biscuits, cheese, peppermints and Nahanni water elegantly served by Bryn on a fuel drum.

Since it was very often impossible to find anywhere safe to beach the boats, all refuelling was done on the move. This was possible by quickly switching the fuel feed pipe between the two five-gallon fuel tanks lashed down by the engine transom. Filling a tank through a funnel when cavorting through a rough patch usually led to considerable fuel spillage and fumes rising from the bilge which slopped about our feet. This meant no smoking in the boats. On an earlier expedition in the Sudan, I had watched a burning photographer run around in blind screaming pain: his hands and legs were soaked in petrol whilst filling a cooker and someone had lit a match somewhere. It all happened so quickly and it was easy to be wise after the event.

Jack McConnell shared my touchiness on the No Smoking rule; the tender area along the inside of his legs had been badly burned a few years before when his dungarees, impregnated with petrol, had ignited whilst he was working in a tank.

For twenty miles the Nahanni snaked through hilly forest, running fast so that our engines laboured against the current at full throttle on the bends but the boats stayed still. In such places we zigzagged, searching for eddies and bounced up and down to help the props bite the water.

None of the boats were planing and most of the time each engine used a gallon a mile which was double the anticipated average and boded ill for chances of reaching the Falls.

The sun beat down and the river ran by a sheer cliff pitted with the holes of swallows. The excrement from each hole's occupants had marked a white line running down the rockface into the hole below which, as Bryn remarked, revealed an anti-social trait among these lovely little birds. The wiser birds doubtless lived in the upper row of holes and so could safely sun themselves on their doorsteps without danger of being blessed by their neighbours from above. The cliff ran along the northern bank and at length the river narrowed as it entered the gorge of the Tlogotsho Mountains.

Ahead lay the first great canyon of the Nahanni but first we stopped at a log cabin in a clearing where the forest lapped at the canyon walls. We wished to see the strange sulphur pools that rise close by, causing a powerful odour which can be smelled five miles away if the wind is right.

Seven very large Canadian youths were occupying the cabin, sleeping all over the floor, so we put our tents in the long grass beside the building. They seemed to have been expecting us, having heard on their radio of our departure from Fort Liard. They were working for a high-powered mining interest but none would tell us what they were after nor what they had found. They had been dropped by a helicopter which took them up into the mountains each day until dusk. Their wiry leader was a friendly man called Cliff James who showed us a 45-gallon drum of fuel which he said was a gift for us from the mining company called Penaroyya. With luck, he said, their helicopter might also have dropped a second drum for us just past the giant rock known as the Pulpit. This was welcome news for our engines were gulping down fuel and would probably use even more in the rapids of the canyons ahead.

The prospectors' guide was half-Indian, a young man named Mickey Kraus whose father had built the cabin many years ago using water from the hot springs to heat the shack in the winter. The Nahanni never freezes where the springs empty their steaming blue water into the main river, even when the general temperature falls to seventy degrees below freezing point.

These pools support a sub-tropical micro-climate to the north of the Arctic Circle: brightly coloured butterflies flit among the colombine that colours the woods and even humming-birds from distant Brazil spend their summer here. These little Calliopes make nests of sphagnum moss bound together with pilfered spider's webs. Their fledglings are no bigger than pennies and the nests are only two inches in diameter; like small tennis balls. The birds can fly backwards and sideways like a helicopter and have acceleration and braking capabilities which would make a Lotus Elan blush. Despite the whirring speed of their little wings their maximum is about twenty-five miles per hour so it must take quite a while to complete their annual trip to Brazil for their winter holiday and back again each summer.

The pools themselves were small but warm with fizzy bubbles rising invitingly to the surface so that Stanley muttered reverently about Devon cider and Joe about Glenfiddich with a touch of soda.

We floated in the pool and washed away the sweat and engine grease with handfuls of sulphurous mud.

Within an hour of our bath, Stanley was back at work on the engines and soon reverted to his earlier mulatto shade. The spare engine which Ginnie had sent us at the Butte had proved useless, since it had a broken throttle cable pivot. Using some piping from the cabin, doctored with our hacksaw blade, Mickey Kraus managed to replace the pivot by two o'clock in the morning. Afterwards we sat by the embers of the camp fire with mugs of hot chocolate enlivened by medicinal brandy. Mickey told us that recently in the wood by the sulphur pools he had surprised two grizzly bears having a picnic on the wild strawberries: he had retired gracefully hoping that the strawberries were to be the bears' dessert rather than their *hors-d'œuvre*. He told us of an unusual happening at the remote Penaroyya silver lead mine on Prairie Creek. The foreman there was a wild-looking man who called himself the Meanest Sonofabitch in the Valley and looked the part. He owned an Alsatian which he allowed to roam at will in the vicinity of the mine. A wolf bitch from the local park had gone lame during the winter and according to wolfish custom was left to fend for herself. Spring came and she got itchy pants, as Mickey put it; a state of affairs which was soon noticed by the foreman's Alsatian who deserted him and befriended the lame she-wolf. The strangely assorted pair were often seen together in the mountains around the mining camp. They have doubtless reared a fine family of young huskies that will terrorise the local caribou for many years.

Mickey told us of the trouble his father had had constructing the cabin because of the sulphurous vapour from the pools which corrodes metal nails and rots wood. Only small plants and shrubs grow in their immediate vicinity and timber for the cabin never lasts very long unless extremely well varnished.

'There must be heavy rain away west,' said Mickey as the fire died down. 'Look at the river. She's come up three feet or more since dusk and those logs are a sure sign of high water above the Falls. You'll not get through George's nor the Gate if the water rises much more. You should have come in August: there's less water then and the rapids are lower.'

Mickey smoothed long fingers against his jawline. His high cheekbones spoke of Indian blood though there was plenty of Prussian gristle in the firm bridge of his nose.

He pointed to the silvery swirl of the river.

'I have seen great standing waves taller than me between here and the cliffs, and the water as thick with debris as carrion with flies. Pa and I could not sleep for fear of the river flooding over its banks. At night I'd listen to the giant logs grind against each other and against the cliff and I'd think there must be better places to live than here. But then after some days the danger would pass and I'd be happy again that this was our cabin.'

Mickey chuckled to himself at his memories. I liked him. Sometimes half-breeds are like many small men, noisy and keen always to justify themselves, but Mickey was quiet, unassuming and genuinely proud of his heritage—the wild river and dark forests of his youth.

The water rose several feet that night and we watched with apprehension as the swirling waters plucked hard at our boat moorings. As soon as the craft were stowed we left, soon engulfed by the great canyon. The towering walls acted as an echo chamber to every gush and twirl of the torrent, the sky narrowed to a faraway strip of blue and we moved in deep shadow: three little ants struggling pathetically against the flow in a sheer-sided drain.

The RFD and the C-Craft managed to navigate the bottleneck of the first sharp bend within the canyon. Here a sandbank to the right narrowed the navigable channel to a choppy chute that hugged the left-hand cliff, spray flying high where successive surging waves dashed against the rock. But the riverboat, with both engines at full throttle and Ben's square chin thrust out aggressively defying the Nahanni, wallowed hopelessly in the lower reaches of the rapid with waves spilling over her bows.

Ben could not turn around in order to withdraw from the rapid as she would have capsized once broadside to the river; so he reduced power carefully and slid back into an eddy.

Hours later we had lightened Ben's load of fuel by ferrying the drums through the rapids in the inflatables: a slow and tricky process. Two hundred gallons lighter, our riverboat, already nicknamed *Torrey Canyon*, ploughed heavily through the bottleneck with Richard bailing like an animated bilge-pump and Paul filming the one-sided competition between his producer and the incoming water.

My diary of that first day in the canyons is brief and not very explicit: 'The river has an unpredictable power of its own. There is little inclination to relax and enjoy the fantastic scenery . . . to do so would be as suicidal as studying the Arc de Triomphe whilst driving around it.'

High above the river soared the sheer red walls, with successive pine-clad tiers of rock teetering atop the lower cliffs; a wild jumbled place where exposed pressure lines of many-hued mineral strata zigzag from ledge to ledge, up to an ice-blue sky. A thin shuddering ribbon of light was reflected in the water, but the sun seldom touched us as we crept along the gloomy corridors of the canyon.

Echoes of turbulence often reached us ahead of the rougher stretches but at Lafferty's Riffle there was no audible warning, only a high-flung spray cresting the river's horizon. Here a fierce rush of water marked the confluence of Lafferty Creek and the Nahanni. Below the mouth of the creek was a crescent-shaped shingle bar which forced the main stream through a narrow channel between the bar and the opposing cliffs.

Again the rubber craft planed their way, bucking madly through the waves only to find that the riverboat could no more than nibble at the lower swell.

Chanting a far-fetched heaving ditty which, according to Jack and Joe, is often crooned by Scots mothers 'to keep the greetin' bairns quiet', we pulled in unison on two long towlines fixed on to our *Torrey Canyon*'s bows.

The song, in case a reader of this narrative should ever find himself in a similar situation, outvoiced by Scotsmen, and wanting something rhythmic to heave to, goes thus:

73

Three craws sa' upon a wa', sa' upon a wa'
sa' upon a wa'a-a-a-a
Three craws sa' upon a wa' on a cauld and frosty morning.

Follow-up verses, all of which are similarly chorused, run:

First craw coodna flay at a', coodna flay at a', etc.
Second craw craw-ed for his maw, craw-ed for his maw, etc.
Third craw up and flayed awa', up and flayed awa', etc.

By the time we had sung ourselves sick of crows, the riverboat was halfway through the rapids, our hands were raw from tugging at the thin wet rope and we had reached a temporary impasse as our exhausted efforts were no longer a match for the current. More brain was required now that the reserves of brawn were depleted.

A small spit of shingle lay on the fringe of the wildest stretch of the rapid and only fifteen yards from our sandbank. Using poles for balance we waded out to the spit, the water tearing at our thighs. Stanley nearly disappeared altogether but made it by partially swimming.

With four on either side of the boat, she responded better, and came finally to the upper end of the spit. Here it was too shallow to use the engines and yet too deep to stand easily without being swept away. Everyone moved back to the sandbar and six of us heaved on a single line whilst Stanley manned the tiller, waiting for sufficient depth to start the motors. Straining hard against the dead weight of the boat we moved into ever deepening and faster water; but still the propellers touched the riverbed.

Ben was the strongest of us, built like a slightly overweight Aberdeen Angus, and when he slipped we all went. It was very sudden, the water was icy and the rope ripped away, burning and tearing the palms of our hands.

The 30-foot riverboat was broadside on now to the main current and moving out towards the rapids. Stanley acted quickly and was lucky, for both motors started immediately once in deep water, stemming the current in reverse.

Swimming and scrabbling for the shelving sandbar, we groped

for the rope and leant back to take the strain as the boat reached the end of the rope's length. With consummate skill, Stanley reversed the boat very slowly upstream, holding her as close to the sandbar as was possible without scraping the propellers.

We were through the Nahanni's first major obstacle and the boats seemed to sense our determination to keep going for even the *Torrey Canyon* held her own as the canyons widened above Lafferty's.

I suppose, subconsciously at any rate, I had been preparing myself for early problems with the boats. We were certainly not out of danger for many worse rapids lay ahead, but at least we were progressing and, once past Lafferty's, we averaged four knots, a fuel consumption rate which would get us to Deadmen Valley although possibly not beyond, where the current was said to speed up.

The little C-Craft edged beside us: someone had painted *Oor Wee Darlin'* on its bows. Jack was sprawled sleeping atop the bulging mummy-bag and Joe yelled above the din of our engines. There was an eager glint in his eyes as he pointed ahead.

'Awa by the forest. Just watch that water jump!'

He ended the observation with a sound I presumed to be the Skibinski clan warwhoop. It was a variation of the noise a cowboy makes when bronco-busting, and the raucous Yipee of a Celtic supporter when the Rangers' goal is threatened. Its effect on Jack was immediate: he awoke with a jerk that nearly had him overboard.

Ahead lay the terminal gorge of the First Canyon where the river rushed violently through a bottleneck called George's Riffle. It was perhaps a mile from us and the cresting waves were clearly visible.

Landing below the white water, we inspected the Riffle carefully. Having heard many tales of disaster resulting from ill-chosen routes through George's, our three helmsmen conferred earnestly with much gesturing and shouting in one another's ears to make themselves heard above the overall cacophony.

The rubber boats went first: it was exhilarating but frightening. The waves were large and came at us from both flanks so that the crews found themselves moving quickly from side to side to transfer their weight. The roar of the motors under full power went unheard, the shock of intermittent drenchings as waves broke over our prows, and the speed with which the boats plunged and climbed, all over, it seemed, in a moment of time. Then we were through and unscrewing the bilge plugs to drain the craft.

Looking back we saw the *Torrey Canyon* — a momentary glimpse of Ben Usher's face thrown up above the highest wave before it disappeared; then the square green bows with their jutting Sampson post broke high in a spume of flying spray to vanish altogether.

When a riverboat, already heavily laden, fills with water, it becomes impossible to steer in such wild water as George's Riffle: it will turn sideways to the flow and overturn if the helmsman loses control even briefly. Great was our relief then when the old boat lurched drunkenly through and chugged on up to join us. That night, camped on an island above the Riffle, Joe found a message in a bottle which told how a group of Americans in a 24-foot jet-powered boat had smashed against a rock in George's and somehow survived their shipwreck to camp on the island. What later befell them was not chronicled by the bottled message.

After George's, the canyon walls fell away. We were in a world of distant valleys, rolling pine-clad hills, and wide white-stoned creeks. This was the legendary Deadmen Valley. Away to the west lay the Headless Mountains and the Funeral Range. Glancing at the map, Bryn Campbell commented that the cartographer must have been a relative of Alfred Hitchcock. There was, in fact, a certain incongruity in the macabre names given to the salient features of the region since it was the most pleasing, almost cheerful, area of the Nahanni we had seen: certainly far less grim than the First Canyon.

The valley was ten miles wide. Somewhere to the west the river squeezed through two more canyons but there was no sign of them from the tiny forest cabin where we camped.

Stanley celebrated his birthday by changing the oil in all the gearboxes: Joe caught three trout, the biggest being ten (Scottish) inches in length. He cooked the fish, and a small rabbit which he had shot, with great care and divided the mixture into eight portions. The cabin must have been built quite recently for it was sound, with few chinks in the log walls. There was, however, a gaping rent in the roof where a 60-foot pine tree had crashed down in a gale. We removed the tree and Ben repaired the roof with ingenuity.

Stanley set to work with the hammer and file in an ambitious effort to reshape the fifteen propellers which we had already buckled. Four had at least one blade missing and one had no blades at all. Damage to propellers can easily be prevented by using a brass, instead of steel, sheerpin to fasten the prop to its shaft. Then, as soon as the propeller meets tough resistance, the pin sheers and disengages the prop from its drive-shaft, saving it from almost any damage.

If we had used brass sheerpins it is true that Stanley would not have had fifteen grossly distorted props to contend with. On the other hand we would not in all likelihood have reached the Hot Springs at all, let alone Deadmen Valley. With heavily laden rubber boats it is vital to maintain power and steerage if there is any danger of snags in the river or along the banks. Drifting out of control in these waters would quickly have led to disaster. Each time we had buckled a blade or two, we'd been able to continue under reduced power until we found a suitable landing place to replace the damaged prop.

While Stan hammered away, Ben stripped naked, crooned a love song, and had a bath in our largest cookpot. I had noticed that the three soldiers, perhaps in a reaction to long years of short back 'n sides, had all sprouted long hair and fuzzy facial fungus as soon as possible. But Ben shaved every day and always looked immaculate despite the heat and the insects. Discipline amongst the British, or anyway the North Yorks, Constabulary must be of a high and lasting order.

I crossed the river in the little Scottish boat and went with the crew to find rabbits beyond Prairie Creek. We followed the stream inland for an hour and smelled the stench of sulphur pools, though we saw none. Moving through a tall forest in dark undergrowth, we heard a roar from higher up the valley: perhaps it was a bear or a cougar, we didn't know and, finding no rabbits, I returned to the cabin leaving Jack and Joe to fish with their handlines.

77

Canadian newspapers have frequently put the Headless Valley's death toll as high as twenty-nine men, all of whom apparently disappeared in circumstances of mystery. I think this figure is unlikely. After careful checking available records and the Royal Geographical Society's library we could trace only seventeen unexplained deaths or disappearances, as well as three straightforward cases of drowning and one plane crash.

The press has poo-pooed the mystery angle from time to time, pointing out that the Nahanni is no place for tenderfeet, that there are plenty of natural hazards like grizzlies, or dying of starvation, that skulls, being spherical, may have rolled two hundred yards into the river. The fact remains, however, that most of these missing men were hardened prospectors who had spent much of their lives surviving in the far north. And it is curious that, though there are a thousand other equally remote and hostile valleys in the north where far greater numbers of prospectors live from year to year, there are no other regions half as rich in tales of death and burnt-out cabins.

*   *   *

The catalogue of disasters begins in the late nineteenth century, when thousands of Canadians, Americans, and Europeans migrated to the Klondike in search of easy money. There were many routes to the goldfields and a few groups, hoping perhaps to avoid the better-known but crowded trails, went up the Nahanni. None of them ever emerged to the west nor indeed returned to the east. Travel writer Raymond Patterson found a possible explanation of their fate: somewhere in Deadmen Valley in 1928 he found decaying remains of temporary cabins of the type made by the Klondikers: perhaps these people contracted an epidemic and died before they could attempt to return to civilisation.

At the turn of the century many prospectors roamed the unexplored valleys of the north-west seeking gold. First there were the burnt and beheaded McLeod brothers and Weir (see chapter 3, page 52), then in 1916 a Mounted Policeman called Corporal Churchill found the headless skeleton of a prospector named Jorgensen up the Nahanni.

The man had been a tough experienced woodsman and his remains were found by a log cabin near the Flat River's confluence with the Nahanni. A loaded rifle was close to the body and the cabin had been burnt down. The police closed the case, stating that it was 'hopeless at this late date to try and establish a cause'. It is difficult to rule out foul play. However heavy a sleeper Jorgensen was he would surely have woken in the burning cabin – if he had been alive.

All police records of events in the area over the next twelve years were destroyed, but in 1922 a prospector named John O'Brien went up the Nahanni and perished. His body was not located by the police as they did not mount a search patrol. Another prospector, Angus Hall disappeared without trace five years later in the same area, and Phil Powers, also a prospector, was found in 1932 by a Mountie patrol. Constable Martin located the charred logs of Powers's cabin upstream of the Flat River mouth and he probed carefully amongst the ashes. He reported finding charred bones in the general outline of a human being laid out on the remains of a bunk as though the man had been sleeping. The skull was still at the opposite end to the footbones and a rifle was found near the knees.

For four years all was quiet in Nahanni country until 1936 when William Epler and Joseph Mulholland, trapping and prospecting along the Nahanni, disappeared without a trace. A pilot named Dalziel located their cabin but reported to Constable Graham at Fort Liard that it had been burnt to the ground. Four years later a prospector named Holmberg was found dead of no established cause.

Early in 1961 Alec Mieskonen was prospecting for gold and was blown up by dynamite: his death was considered to be suicide despite his well-known fear of explosives; his two partners Orville Webb and Tom Pappas set off overland for Nahanni Butte since they were running short of food: they were never seen again.

The following year the pilot of a crashed aeroplane disappeared in the Headless Valley. Blake Mackenzie was a strong healthy man and his plane was later located with an ample supply of food close to the river. His diary was also found which showed that he was alive and well forty-two days after the crash. Then, abruptly and inexplicably, the daily notes ceased and Mackenzie was never found.

The scoffers had a ready explanation for Mackenzie's disappearance. Why: he had simply faked the whole thing in order to disappear conveniently for personal reasons.

The same year another small plane crashed in the Headless Valley and a prospector named Hudson was found dead by the plane. The fate of the pilot and the other two occupants is not known since there was no sign of them.

For a remote river valley into which relatively few people have ventured, this death list is formidable. Looking through the 1961 quarterly magazine of the Royal Canadian Mounted Police I found a detailed summary of the finding of the Nahanni corpses, nearly all of whom had been prospectors. The writer, Police Constable Shaw, ended the report with the remark:

Of the deaths recorded here — overlooking Weir's and O'Brien's which police did not investigate — there is one aspect common to all which appears to have been overlooked by the myth-makers. Take a quick look over the account of each of these deaths and you will find that fire of undetermined origin has been a factor in each in some way or other . . .

Remembering the tone of this report I was especially interested by a story told me by Brian Doke at Nahanni Butte. Brian's father-in-law, Mr Turner, had travelled up the Nahanni eight years before to take some food to a man whose cabin was further upriver. Brian could not remember whether the fellow was a prospector or a trapper or both, but he did remember that Mr Turner had found him dead on his bunk and the cabin burnt down about him. The story never made headlines, possibly because the dead man's head was firmly intact.

We heard tales of Spanish galleons shipwrecked on the rocky coastline of British Columbia with 'cargoes of apes'. The theory was that some of these apes escaped ashore and headed inland. The long

The lone sentinel rock at the Gate of the Nahanni. Though it towers for hundreds of feet above the river, it is dwarfed by the sheer cliffs of the Second Canyon.

The Scotsmen pan for gold at the mouth of the Flat River where the bodies of the 1964 Expedition were found. The distinct colours of the two rivers are plainly visible.

Spotting potential routes between the twin cauldrons of the Figure of Eight Rapids.

winters killed off all but a few who, finding hot sulphurous springs somewhere in the Nahanni region, survived over the years and were the cause of the various decapitations.

In October 1920 a young Canadian geologist James Watts, returned from a hunting trip in the valleys of the South Nahanni. He said that he had met some of the shy Nahanni Indians who told a strange tale of huge prehistoric monsters and white cannibals who raided them from time to time. Watts had thought this must be fiction until the Indians drew pictures of monsters on deerskins which were similar to prehistoric mastodons and mammals known to have roamed the muskegs and forests of the sub-Arctic. This may sound like a tall traveller's tale but there are also stories about the sasquatch or North American model of the Himalayan yeti. The sasquatch is also known as the bigfoot owing to its 16-inch footprints which have been found along with samples of excreta and hair. American universities have analysed these samples and confirmed that they come from no known mammal. Bob Angus, the editor of the Fort Nelson newspaper, has reports and a photograph of a seven-foot-tall furry creature standing in the forest. Bob told us that a trapper at Nahanni Butte had given him the photograph after seeing the beast twice in different areas. We later met the trapper in question, but he refused to be drawn on his experience. Yet even if a few shy and almost extinct sasquatches do conceivably prowl the western region of North America, they are traditionally vegetarian, and have never attacked the few human beings who have reported meeting them.

Most remote areas of the world have their mystery animals, their kaptars, mehtehs and abominable snowmen. And there are the undeniably authentic photographs of the giant yeti footprints taken by Eric Shipton's Everest expedition on the Menlung glacier. These prints show toes that are inverted like a gorilla's, rather than the straightforward humanoid toes of the North American bigfoot. Many reports tell of female sasquatches with 'well-developed hairy breasts and good childbearing hips'. 'The mind boggles,' commented Bryn. 'I bet the randy old trappers up here never had it so good.'

Before summarily dismissing the sasquatch to the realms of

mythology, it is well to remember that only 150 years ago anthropologists were scoffing at reports of the gorilla, which was unknown to civilised man until the 1840s; and scientifically there is no reason why yetis should not exist any more than underwater monsters or UFOs. But—despite analysed yeti dung, ciné-films, and the reports of a thousand and one non-alcoholic witnesses—there has as yet been no conclusive proof brought to light of the existence of these friendly zombies who excite the imagination of lonely hikers from the Arctic to the Tropics.

* * *

Before and beyond Deadmen Valley the mountains closed in about the Nahanni but by the cabin the river flowed in such a way that a small seaplane could land without difficulty. On our second day in the valley, a Beaver floatplane owned by Steve Villars roared over us.

Jack spoke to the circling plane on his tiny Sarbe radio, describing the wind conditions and the location of some floating snags large enough to buckle a seaplane's floats. There was no reply but the Beaver landed neatly and taxied upstream to our bank.

With Steve was Moira Farrow, a *Vancouver Sun* reporter whom we had met in Edmonton. The *Sun* was to get exclusive reports in exchange for payment of the high freight charges of the fuel that Steve brought with him in fourteen ten-gallon drums.

So long as the extra forty-five gallons, promised us by the Penaroyya mining concern had been dropped as planned at the Pulpit Rock, we should now have enough fuel to reach the Falls.

Ginnie had persuaded Steve that, since she weighed less than four jerrycans of fuel, she should accompany Moira. Thoughtfully she had brought eight T-bone steaks, fresh milk and some insect repellent. Every evening with Corporal Wallace, she had visited a derelict fire-watch tower in Fort Nelson with the radio and listened for our signals. Three hundred miles of forest and a double range of lofty mountains had precluded radio contact but they had listened every day nonetheless.

Ginnie and I wandered off. She was curious to know how the men were getting on together as a team. I told her that the soldiers were strong, keen and reliable. That Bryn was cheerful, never at loss for a joke and seemingly unperturbed by his near-drowning. He slept, ate and thought with the Army. The BBC film team and I were bickering a bit, but only mildly, it was not like an earlier expedition I'd been on when the photographers had lived apart from the rest, building up such underlying tension that it had ended in violence.

It was inevitable really that there would be a certain amount of difference between the BBC team and myself, for our aims were in partial conflict. I had a schedule to keep which involved completing a certain mileage each day, and this meant dawn reveilles, no lunch stops and late-night halts. I was afraid that getting behind schedule would mean extreme cold and danger on the Fraser River in October and I feared that we might run out of rations on the Nahanni. Richard Robinson, as film producer, wanted more rest for his cameraman, Paul Berriff, whose filming he said would otherwise suffer. He wanted to start at eight, stop for an hour or more at midday and camp for an hour before sundown. I felt there was no need to halt at midday as dehydrated biscuits and cheese taste just as good on the move and in this heat cold water was as satisfying as hot tea. Also the BBC men would have liked less monotonous food. They still remembered the sumptuous provisions they had had on their previous assignment in the Grand Canyon. As it was, they supplemented their rations with Fortum and Mason-type goodies which were all extra weight.

Ginnie asked me about Constable Ben. I couldn't fathom him out at all. He seemed to be a dour Yorkshireman with his head screwed firmly on. He listened to Richard when it suited him and often treated Paul like a child. The three of them spent their time complaining about one thing or another and Richard was their spokesman but I sometimes got the idea that Ben would have been quite reasonable if not pushed by the other two. Paul was young and headstrong but marvellously professional. When he was filming he forgot his surroundings completely. I had watched him filming on the Butte when his hands were grey with mosquitoes. He let them drink and kept panning the camera steady as a rock. His camera was never out of reach and he was unusually observant.

Richard, I knew, felt sure that I saw the film team as a necessary evil. Without them and the resulting publicity for the equipment we used I would not have been able to afford the expedition. But one could only admire their sheer professionalism. They were superb at their job and nothing was too much effort for them if it helped with the filming.

Someone was shouting from the direction of the river, so we walked back. Ginnie climbed into the little cockpit, and the seaplane was soon visible only as a silvery glint on the horizon.

We left the Valley soon after dawn the following day. Since the current ahead would be stronger than anything yet experienced, we put the two good Evinrudes on the *Torrey Canyon* and the older engine to power the C-Craft which carried only minimal equipment and Jack McConnell at the helm.

The river widened within the Valley and soon rushed headlong through the scattered debris and gravel bars of a low flood plain, not unlike the Splits.

Jack fired some shots and we turned cautiously amidst a tangle of moving sweepers to go back to his rescue. He was cartwheeling helplessly, his engine inoperative, and gathering speed as the swirling water sucked the C-Craft towards a cluster of threshing roots.

Three times Stanley swooped close to Jack who threw me his line. Each time I missed the snaking rope which splashed into the river beyond my reach. We were also perilously close to the sweepers and ducked to avoid the slash of low branches. Then I caught the line and fastened it to a cleat on the transom. For a while we lost ground to the fierce pull of the river, then, helped by a contrary eddy, the engine achieved maximum grip and we inched slowly upstream hardly daring to glance to either side where great tree trunks crashed. I remember hoping that no shallow reef would snare our propeller for then we would all drown.

We landed by a sandbar on the T-junction of three channels. The

84

Torrey Canyon's transom board was split across its entire width and leaking fast, for the bows were aground.

There had been an old axe at the cabin in Deadmen Valley and presumably some nails were lying about the place. There was now no alternative but to return there and attempt repairs for all our heavy equipment and two-thirds of the precious fuel supply were on the riverboat whose entire rear transom was split and about to crack away from the rest of its framework. Ben Usher was only able to apply half throttle to the motors; and even then the resulting downward strain on the transom threatened to tear it apart.

Back at the log cabin, Stanley wormed a number of long nails from the walls and door, long redundant coathangers for some old trapper. There was a thick plywood board in the bows of the river-boat, a panel which stopped the equipment from sliding about. We nailed this across the damaged transom and fixed it at either end to the main sidewalls, using flattened sheets of rusty tin to effect the joins.

Finally a metal rod was passed through both transom boards and bolted to the floor of the boat. Since we had no drill to make a passage for the rod we fired a 7·62 bullet through the wood and widened the bullet-hole further by heating the rod over a fire.

Two hours of careful work with the file thinned the new transom board down to a breadth acceptable to the engine clamps and we tried once again to leave the Valley of Vanishing Men behind us.

5

The Devil's Whirlpool

WHEN THE CANADIAN EXPLORER FENLEY HUNTER REACHED THE great falls on the South Nahanni River, he was followed post-haste by an Indian messenger bearing the news that his wife had just given birth to a daughter. The parents had agreed in advance that a girl would be called Virginia, so the explorer named the Falls in her honour. To reach the Virginia Falls we had to go up what the American Colonel Snyder had described as 'the fastest river in America and the most dangerous in five continents'. It meant our motors must average less than a gallon a mile, and as we approached the dark bastion of the Second Canyon, it was already evident, after a long slow struggle through the flood plain, that we might run out of fuel well short of our objective.

Stanley brought the silver boat into a strip of shingle below the cliffs. When the others joined us after a while, I decided we must disembark the C-Craft and carry it on board the *Torrey Canyon*. It had slowed us down with its temperamental old engine and was using a ridiculous amount of fuel to no avail.

There was much dissent and suggestions that it be towed behind rather than on the riverboat. But that would never work for the C-Craft's drag in the riverboat's wash would be considerable and almost certainly slow the latter craft down to the point where it lost headway. I was adamant and started to haul the C-Craft aboard myself, for there was no time to be lost in discussion.

The great river roared through the canyon with frightening power using even the smallest rock outcrop or curve in the canyon walls as an excuse to form violent eddies. There was nowhere to camp in safety, only low-lying sandbars which might well find themselves below twelve feet of water overnight. Firewood was sparse here and we were cold from the spray. The sun had long since passed behind the rim of the canyon making the place gloomy and a chill river breeze blew off the wet rock about us so we pushed on.

The *Torrey Canyon* was not noticeably affected by the extra weight of the C-Craft and soon after dusk we came to a little island. It was densely wooded so the insects were bad but a stack of timber waste was soon blazing and our wet clothes hung over branches near the fire. My socks were both roasted that evening and my feet went straight through their soles the next day, reminding me of a friend's trousers which I had once destroyed the same way whilst camping in Norway. He had looked most elegant for the next few days hiking in shirt, underpants, and hobnail boots.

Ben Usher had a bath in the largest of our billy cans: his rear end fitted into the pot by a narrow margin and a wager was taken as to whether he would be able to remove himself unaided when the time came. He had a good voice and crooned ecstatically during his frequent bathing sessions.

Almost immediately after the Second Canyon fell away from the river the cliffs of a third and greater canyon loomed ahead and we came to the notorious maw of the Nahanni known as the Gate. The sheer ramparts of scarred limestone to the south climb in a single giant slab to well over 2,000 feet and dwarf the rock which juts like a shark's tooth from the river.

This crumbling sentinel, itself over three hundred feet high, glints with some black metallic substance, and stands where the river is narrowest and the current exceptionally powerful. In high spring water the place must be a nightmare to navigate. At full throttle we made little impression on the current, swinging sideways in the grip of the great eddies which boil the water's surface and move almost as fast as the main torrent, but in the opposite direction.

Beyond the Gate, where the river curves to the west, a clear creek tumbles down a rocky ravine. We stopped by the mouth of the creek and searched for the fuel drum that the Penaroyya helicopter was to have left there. There was no sign of it, nor footprints in the sand between the round white boulders of the creek.

It was an idyllic place and morale was high for we knew the Falls were within our grasp as the fuel situation was better now with only three engines running. It was easy to forget the Devil's Whirlpool and the five-mile rapids below the waterfall, for here, by the Gate, the sun shone and we swam in deep cool eddies; relaxing out of reach of the voracious horseflies.

Stanley tinkered with his beloved engines whilst the two Scotsmen climbed to the summit of the cliffs with the radio and dipole aerial. Bryn went too, festooned with cameras.

On the beach above my pool the sun glinted on the bald patch of Richard's head which nodded as he scribbled vigorously in his script book. From away behind our tents echoed shouts and splashes from the creek where Ben and Paul were washing. That evening they saw a cougar chase a squirrel which escaped up a tree and Jack later told us of a large black bear which he had watched ambling through some bush. We heard the heavy scuffling of animals at night but the bears never bothered us.

Thunder rolled in the west during the night but the rain held off and by noon the next day we had passed through the hazardous shallows which lie in the region of the Nahanni's confluence with the Flat River. Where the rivers join, it seemed easier to bear left but the water changed from brown to blue-green and the muddy Nahanni curved right around a sandbar which — though less obvious — was the correct route.

In the shallow eddies where the two rivers met we panned for gold, shaking the large ladle in the approved Klondike fashion until the gold was topmost in the silt. Joe came away with almost an ounce of the tiny flakes which we later discovered were 'fool's gold', so-called because it closely resembles the real stuff but is valueless.

My knuckles ached from sounding the river hour after hour; the skin on my hands was greenish and withered like old apple peel from day-long immersion in the icy water. Two propellers buckled on reefs that evening despite our caution and a storm broke as we came to the acute bend in the river which causes the phenomenon of the Devil's Whirlpool.

A sandbar island lay between us and the whirlpools, hiding a low beach rimmed by forest. We pitched camp as high above the beach as the rising ground allowed in pouring rain.

'We could be in danger here,' Stan shouted above the din of the storm. 'It's only about eight feet down to the beach and the river might rise quite a bit tonight.' He reckoned it would be better to attempt the whirlpools that evening, before the ever-growing volume of water increased their power any more. And if we made it through them, we might find a higher and safer camping place upstream.

But I thought of the Germans who had drowned here. It would be wrong to try the passage without first learning the pattern of the water's behaviour, and assessing a way to avoid the suction of the whirlpools.

Jack checked the river level before we turned out the torch in our tent. It had risen three feet in two hours and was coming up fast. We were still some five feet above water level and certainly not keen to move the tents and equipment further up the bank, even if there had been anywhere else flat enough for a camp.

Inertia had set in and a certain tinge of apprehension caused by the awe with which people had spoken of the whirlpools. The rain drummed solidly on the tent, so that intermittent trickles soaked through the canvas and dribbled onto our sleeping-bags in the dark. I tried to roll my knees up to my chest for warmth but it was impossible, for we were five in a four-man tent and to adopt any position other than the fully prone was liable to tear down all our delicately hung mosquito nets and cause much chaos and cursing.

Above the sound of the deluge and the crash of great pines in the gale, the faint fluctuating boom of waves in the Devil's Whirlpool was plainly audible. I lay awake with my hands tucked under their opposing armpits for warmth and tried to visualise how the Germans had drowned. At some stage I must have fallen asleep for I next remember waking from a dream in which I had been drowning slowly. But there were no boats in the dream: I was in a slimy pit with many snakes and hornets all of which were swimming towards me—though hornets are not naturally swimmers so far as I know— and I was climbing a rope, desperately trying to escape the serpents and the hornets. I never seemed to tire and climbed hand over hand without effort, but always the water rose as fast as I climbed and always the creatures were a little closer. Then the water began to rise faster and soon I was climbing beneath the water and suffocating so that I could no longer climb faster than the snakes and one slithered wetly against my cheek and I awoke.

It was cold and the pullover under my head was wringing wet from a leak in the tent. I looked out of the tent to see the river no more than three feet below the level of our camp. But the rain had stopped and the eight of us soon clambered through dripping foliage and moved along what may once have been an ancient portage trail towards the sound of the rapids.

A man could spend many hours watching the Devil's Whirlpool, trying to learn the pattern of its moving teeth, and come away none the wiser. There are two distinct whirlpools of immense power and at times quite close to one another. Situated on an acute bend in the course of the river, they are caused by the solid rock apex of the curve which takes the full force of the descending water and turns it back upon itself in turmoil.

Looking upstream, the river traveller is faced with sheer cliffs on either side which overhang the river that has gouged out caverns in their base over the years. The first thing to avoid was obviously the danger of being drawn into these caverns and scraped up and down their walls by the recurrent waves that break there.

To the far side of the Nahanni, on the inner flank of the river's hinge, the way was barred by the high standing wave which reached from the cliff to the further of the two whirlpools.

We must take a mid-river course, away from either cliff but avoiding the whirlpools. This would not have been too difficult had the pools remained constant in their size and location, but, as we watched, the twin maws gyrated across the whole width of the river, sometimes slowly, sometimes with speed so that the water tripped over itself forming subsidiary whirlpools and great boils that spread away from the central violence like tidal waves from an undersea eruption.

Stanley, Ben and the Scotsmen, agreeing that there was no sure passage through the hazard, set up a Schermuly safety line across the river, which would hang low enough above the water to be grabbed after a capsize or engine failure, providing the crewmen were not sucked downwards immediately.

First Stanley went to the other bank by boat below the rapids and positioned himself on the cliff opposite us. Ben then fired a Schermuly rocket, its thin 400-foot line snaking away over the river to where Stanley stood. We attached a 300-foot nylon rope to the rocket line which Stanley then pulled across and made firm to a tree with the line lying above the lower extreme of the whirlpools. Although the rope was perhaps unlikely to prove very helpful in an emergency, it at least gave us Dutch courage and, after a light breakfast of oatmeal biscuits, tea and a Mars Bar we packed the boats and nosed cautiously upriver.

The Scotsmen went first in the lightly laden C-Craft. We watched them intently until the little boat disappeared as though suddenly engulfed. Some seconds later orange anoraks and the entire boat were momentarily visible flung clear above the waves.

Seeing nothing more of the C-Craft, we moved upstream at full throttle. The old RFD hit the lower series of waves at speed and became airborne. We saw the right-hand whirlpool and veered violently left to avoid it. The boat thudded into a pocket of spinning waves and, although moving fast, was tossed sideways, sending us sprawling among the fuel drums. For an age, so it seemed, we lurched crazily between the whirlpools in a watery no-man's-land of eddies converging from either side.

The stern slipped left without warning and we swung into the outer convolutions of the whirlpool. Stanley turned the helm and gathered speed, moving straight towards the overhanging cliff to the left. Our momentum carried us clear of the eye of the whirlpool and, once beyond its drag rings, we veered to our earlier course and so missed the cliffs by a narrow margin.

Soon we were in calmer water above the bend and watched as Ben brought the heavy riverboat through the rapids. Hugging the cliffline with skill for, unlike the rubber craft, he had less reason to fear the submerged reefs that might lie beside the cliffs, he passed well to the left of the central turbulence, and beyond the reach of the whirlpool. He came perilously close to the overhang but angled the bows to avoid the powerful backwash of the cliffs.

Despite the small size of their boat, the Scotsmen had found a way between the whirlpools and had watched our zigzag course with much amusement and contempt as was evident from Joe's remarks when we joined them.

'You're rubbish, so y'are. I'd sooner go over the Falls in our wee boat than down the Tweed in that antique.'

'He who laughs last laughs longest,' retorted Stan. 'Watch your patter or you'll have no one to fix your motor when it next goes wrong.'

The C-Craft crew, checkmated, lapsed into silence and we collected the BBC below the rocky promontary from where they had been filming.

*   *   *

The storm had cleared and the forest steamed, astir with scurrying life busily collecting oddments of food for winter storage or twigs and moss to line a burrow for the long months of hibernation. Chipmunks and ground squirrels often peeked at us in curiosity from leafy perches relatively secure from their natural enemies — the lynx, wolf, coyote, fox, and weasel families and hidden from the deadly aerial predators the eagles, hawks and owls.

The most vicious hunters of the squirrel clans are decidely the weasel tribe which includes the wolverine, a vicious three-foot-long killer with a Latin name meaning 'short-sighted gourmand'. Its favourite activity is to follow an Indian trapline killing and eating the helpless victims caught in the snares. Trappers build high 'dog kennel' food caches on 12-foot stilts, solidly fashioned from logs, where they leave their food and equipment for the coming winter. The wolverine, not to be outdone, climbs the stilts—usually the lopped-off trunks of four conveniently placed trees—and gnaws its way through 10-inch logs. Once inside, it removes the equipment as well as the food and hides everything in a hole. Before leaving its ill-gotten gains it will brand them by spraying foul liquid from its backside into the hole. Only smooth sheets of tin tacked around the cache stilts will keep the wolverine out of a 'dog kennel'.

Equally notorious weasel relatives are the martens and pekan martens. The word marten is derived from Mars, the Roman god of war, and well sums up these bellicose creatures. They have magnificent furs but attempts to start marten farms end in failure since the captive males kill the females and the females kill their own young—an impressive variation on prison hunger-strikes.

The marten can move even faster through the treetops than the red squirrel, though it is naturally out-manœuvred by the flying squirrels. The pekan however is an even more accomplished acrobat and is not averse to catching and killing its brother the marten. Pekans are better known as Fishers which is strange since they never fish.

The true weasel or ermine changes from brown to pure white during the winter months and, unlike its relatives, kills for pleasure more often than hunger. The smallest of all ermines is called the Least Weasel, the little creature which the British Museum were so keen for us to collect.

Even before our arrival in Edmonton, the Canadian papers discovered and disclosed that we were after a Least Weasel and the reporter who flew into the Headless Valley told us that two readers in Vancouver would donate dead weasels to the expedition and so save us the laborious process of trying to catch one. One donor kept his weasel frozen in a fridge, the other kept his stuffed and on the mantelpiece.

*   *   *

93

Beyond the Devil's Whirlpool the river maintained a deceptively smooth character for several miles. There were barely thirty gallons of fuel left for the three motors but it seemed there were only a dozen miles to the waterfall. Father Mary's 'galloping horse' rapids did not materialise until the Nahanni wound snake-like through a series of narrow bends with ever steepening banks.

Soon the mountain walls were tight about the river, the spray off wind-whipped swell soaked us through, and the boats lost headway in a millrace of churning combers.

The *Torrey Canyon* came into her own for, with two engines at full throttle, her weight held her lower in the water where she was affected less by the debilitating action of the breakers on the screws. She rolled past us, two men poling zealously in the bows for Ben held her close to the cliffs, a practice which aided the riverboat greatly by keeping her out of the full force of the current, but was also risky owing to the frequent rockfalls.

Stanley fought with the tiller, trying desperately to hold our craft straight whilst we wallowed about. Bryn shouted from his perch on the mummy-bag. 'The riverboat's in trouble. They've struck something and it looks like they're out of control.'

A long way ahead, I glimpsed the *Torrey Canyon*, broadside on to the Nahanni, waves broke over her so that only the heads of the crew were visible.

There was no time to see more. We had our own problems, for the RFD was creaking under the conflicting strains of cargo weight, maximum engine thrust, and the ceaseless pounding of the waves.

An orange scar I had noticed gashed in the cliff was in just the same place relative to our progress as it had been ten minutes earlier. We were using fuel fast but getting nowhere. To move diagonally or broadside across rapids as violent and powerful as these would be asking for trouble but was the only alternative to this head-on course which would probably hold us at checkmate until we ran out of petrol. And so, as carefully as possible, Stanley began to tack between the waves straightening out only at the last and most hazardous moment as each successive hydraulic broke above us. We plyed the paddles as strongly as we might under the doubtful principle that every little effort helped.

We began to make progress, albeit extremely slowly and after a while, exhausted, we reached a patch of flatter water where we came upon the riverboat. Edging alongside, Jack told us they had struck a reef and badly buckled the propellers. Somehow Ben had managed to get both engines going again while the rest of the crew, two on each side, kept the boat from overturning as it swung to and fro in the rapids. They had taken in much water and were still bailing hard with the gold-panning bowl and other tins.

Our collective fuel supply was low now and I was unsure how far we had come since my waterproofed map had disappeared in the rapids and the spare was packed deep in the mummy-bag.

We idled beside the *Torrey Canyon* for a while as everyone recovered their wind. Despite the rough water behind and ahead of us that sounded above the whine of the motors, I became aware of another greater noise as of unseen but continuous thunder.

For a long while the canyon wound ever deeper into cliffs of ochre limsestone whilst the river raced towards us in overall confusion. I remembered Colonel Snyder's words — 'the fastest river in America and the most dangerous in five continents'. In less than a hundred miles we had climbed over a thousand feet. The riverboat with its buckled propellers was moving as slowly as our RFD now and keeping further from the bank despite the violence of the rapids.

These were taller more purposeful waves than any we had experienced; coming one after the other with a violence that threatened the boat. For the first time I felt completely insecure: perhaps because of the almost animated roar and rush of the water. Each time the craft raced down the backend of a curling hydraulic it felt like a rapidly descending lift and I wondered for a second if the next monster would crash down upon us whilst we wallowed in the trough.

Stanley's zigzag tactics did not work well, but they at least produced a slow sort of progress. Bryn and I were no longer paddling, having sapped our energy. We crouched behind the mummy-bag waiting to jump sideways at the anticipated moment of capsize.

95

Perhaps some long-submerged rockpile stirred the river for, without warning, a great wave came at us conversely from the flank stopping the boat dead under its weight, leaving us in a watery vacuum. Try as we might, the old boat stayed doggedly in this isolated pocket of converging currents, her bows slanting steeply to port and slowly keeling over.

Reacting quickly, Bryn flung himself on the starboard bow and yelled at me to do the same.

The boat responded so sensitively to his weight transference that I lost balance and landed more forcibly on the bows than intended, squashing Bryn flat beneath me.

With our combined weight up front, the frantic whine of cavitation changed to a deeper note as the Evinrude gripped with effect, the boat straightened, and slowly inched up the wall of water which ensnared us. Stanley zigged the tiller and, shouting with relief, we came over the crest in an explosion of spray. After that, everything seemed possible. Nothing could stop us now. Bryn's teeth chattered but he grinned as though he were enjoying life immensely, and began to chant wild and totally unintelligible dirge whilst wringing the water from his fuzzy beard.

Soon reaction began to set in and the wind made itself felt through our soaking anoraks and damp pullovers. We huddled low behind the comparative shelter of the mummy-bag. Stanley remained exposed at the tiller, scanning upstream through bloodshot red-rimmed eyes. He too was shivering and his skin was pale and mottled over his cheekbones. It would be no good asking if he was cold and wanted a rest a while for the answer was always the same. Stanley was never cold or tired when things were bad. Secretly I suspected that he hated the thought of anyone else touching his motor which always ran smoother than the others possibly because Stanley had chosen it himself.

As sunset approached however all thoughts of cold and hunger left us for the sound of pounding water intensified minute by minute to an overall boom that bored deep within the brain.

The source of sound was a massive buttress that reared above us in mid-river as we cleared the final bend. From the sky, or so it

Straining yard by yard through the millrace of the Five Mile Rapids.

The Scotsmen have their first hard-won view of the mighty Virginia Falls.

The Virginia Falls, twice the height of Niagara.

seemed from our water-level viewpoint, there issued an immense waterfall that split in two around the central buttress. The last rays of sunset played along the very rim of the Falls where streamers of high-flung spray sparkled below a rainbow of falling mist.

Ben's sombrero flew high in the air above the *Torrey Canyon*, Paul's camera whirred, recording the expressions on our faces during the moment of success, even Richard showed emotion but our ragged cheer was drowned in the general tumult.

The month-long struggle was over; and what a reward. There are places in South Africa, the Sudan, even Arabia, which had seemed to me at the time more beautiful than anywhere else in the world, but nothing could compare with the sheer inspiration of that first view of the Virginia Falls. That we had striven so hard to get there had much to do with it, and I felt a warmth in my chest, a surge of unidentifiable emotion. For me, and — judging by their expressions — for the others, that moment of arrival, the first sight of that remote waterfall, twice the height of the great Niagara, justified the expedition.

6

Fort Nelson

WE SPENT TWO DAYS CAMPED BY THE FALLS COLLECTING ROCK
specimens for the British Museum. Then we raced back to Nahanni
Butte hurtling along on the full force of the current. It was good to
be going with the flow for a change instead of struggling against it.
Bryn flew off to a job in Europe and the BBC TV crew left to film
fires in British Columbia where 131 major conflagrations were
currently burning throughout the province. We were all to join up
later, meanwhile the three soldiers and I left Nahanni Butte to take
the boats back to Fort Nelson.

*   *   *

The sun's heat fell intense on the Liard River, and the jarring grind
of our motors as they fought the current echoed back from the banks,
inescapable as the heat and the glare. At first we sensed no danger.
Stan was snoring, his bearded chin twitching involuntarily when a
mosquito bit deep. I pulled the tiller over and gave the boat throttle
to avoid a log. Stan slipped off the rubber side-tube, landing amongst
empty fuel drums, but he slept on.

Then Joe Skibinski waved from the other craft, away to the
right, and pointing ahead where the great river's horizon joined the
march of the forest. There was a khaki dimming of the sky, an orange
pall, as of distant city lights by night. But it was noon. I blinked and

gazed again, but still the haze persisted, growing darker as we moved south. In half an hour the sun was covered by a halo, and the river ran a deep ochre. The acrid odour of wood smoke preceded a fine layer of soft grey snowflakes. The heat was stifling. We were 100 miles from anywhere, with fuel for perhaps another twenty. Ahead lay our precious petrol drums. Stan had woken up, but we said nothing. The other boat moved close beside us now; all of us gazing south, the same unspoken thought running through our minds.

A Forest Ranger had warned us that the power and intensity of the great fires is immense. They can jump across two-mile-wide lakes in a matter of minutes and boil the surface water of rivers once the forest is ablaze on both banks. I remembered him telling us that it was easy to get fried—even quicker with fuel drums on board.

The floating ash stung our eyes, making it impossible to see the many sandbanks by their telltale surface ripples. Grimy smears of ash ran down our stomachs and dripped from Stanley's beard onto his tattered khaki trousers.

'I can't see a bloody thing and there's no way of telling how far away the fire is,' he yelled from the tiller. Everything had to be shouted fortissimo as our engine cover had broken some days before when the boat smashed into a cliff descending Lafferty's Riffle. Unmuffled, the engine's roar was deafening. We paused on the bank for the engine was overheating.

Joe sprawled limply in the sticky heat munching wild strawberries. His jaws stopped in mid-munch and he sat bolt upright listening intently.

'D'ye hear that?' he asked of no one in particular, his mouth half open so that he might hear more acutely. 'A sort of distant roar and crackle.'

Jack nodded. 'Aye. It's from the south-west I think. Sometimes it's there and then it's awa' and you canna hear a thing.'

Stanley looked at me; his eyebrows raised enquiringly. I shrugged and shook my head. All I could hear was a perpetual buzz in both ears as if the engine was still running. He was similarly affected and there was no way of telling whether or not the Scotsmen were pulling our legs—as was their wont. But the smoke was growing more dense and the blowing ash falling thicker so, forgetting the motor's well-being, we went our way again, coming with much relief to Nelson Forks soon after dusk.

I was coughing and having trouble with my eyes which watered continuously so that I twice guided Stanley into sandbars which we rammed heavily. The thought of what our last remaining propeller must look like made me wince.

The petrol cache had not been molested and the mosquito population was as hungry as it had been a month earlier.

The air was heavy with menace and our eyes burnt with the acrid smoke. We could not know where the fire advanced nor how fast. The safest course was to gain Fort Nelson as quickly as possible before the fire cut us off. We brewed tea and stew since we had slept little for three days and it would require all our vigilance to navigate by night. Then for five hours we slid south through a strange and silvery gloom, always sounding the water for shallows. The forest seemed to close in about us so that the thin gleaming ribbon of the river was visible only by looking upwards at the moonless sky. That way we could visually sense the river's course: but to scan the blackness ahead directly with the eye was fruitless for then the faint silhouette of water merged into obscurity and there would be the momentary panic of blindness.

My head felt heavy and twice I woke with a start, crouching on the bows. Stanley was feeling weary too. Rather than risk falling overboard in our sleep and being minced efficiently by the 40-horse-power engine, we decided to stop, fire or no fire.

There was no way of telling where best to spend the night so we edged cautiously to the side, struck a partially uprooted tree and moved along its length to the bank. It was twenty foot high and crumbling. The forest above was largely dead and we cleared a small area of soft humus, disturbing many hundreds of small biting insects. Exhausted, we forgot the fire and the gnats and slept deeply.

I was woken by mosquitoes biting my face and shoulders. It was hot and stuffy but the smoke pall had gone so that only the charred sticks and ash swirling in the river told of a fire somewhere. Perhaps it had come close to us but veered away through a change in the prevailing wind: we would never know for certain.

Sixty long miles from our camp site we met a beautifully constructed riverboat with two 55-horse-power motors on her transom. We waved and the helmsman shouted so we beached alongside a muddy clearing.

It was Doctor John Ferries who had written at such length to advise me of the Nahanni's hazards and the limitations of inflatables in such waters. He knew for he had already attempted to reach the Falls using both rubber and riverboats. This time, together with his two sons and some friends he was making a determined effort. He had built the 30-footer himself and towed it by trailer from Vancouver to Fort Nelson.

Later we heard that he had reached the mouth of the Flat River below the Devil's Whirlpool before eventually turning back short of fuel. He sold his riverboat in Fort Simpson and, when we finally met him again in Vancouver, he was as determined as ever to reach the Falls 'one of these days'.

We wolfed down a number of deliciously fresh sandwiches from the Ferries goodies crate whilst they sampled a packet of our dehydrated rations. We thanked them with great sincerity and they us, through politeness rather than appreciation, for as Bryn had once acidly remarked, 'assault rations are delectable so long as one is half-starved and totally lacking in any sense of taste before being subjected to them'.

We shook hands with the riverboat crew and wished them luck. For a long while after we left them, I pondered over Doctor Ferries' advice. He thought that the Nahanni was an adventure indeed but the Fraser was something else altogether for there were more than a hundred major rapids in long narrow canyons; all far worse even than the Devil's Whirlpool. He suggested that to tempt the Fraser in small inflatables was tantamount to suicide.

The Doctor struck me as an eminently sensible man and one who would enjoy the calculated risks of wild-river travel so long as the odds were relatively even. It was his advice more than anything which later influenced much of my thinking in the Fraser canyons where there came to be an awkward choice between the morale or the safety of the expedition.

Meanwhile the engines began to overheat more frequently. The humidity was unusually high, everything was clammy and the leaden heat beat upon the river and the boats. Every few hours, with a conscious effort against increasing lethargy, we moved about the boat letting out air from the hull tubing and from the petrol jerry-bags which became periodically swollen with expanding fumes.

The great drift-pile at 'Bryn's Folly' was no longer evident and a bed of rippling shallows marked the curve where only four weeks before a raging torrent had dashed against the island.

Stanley touched my arm and, following his gaze, I saw the thin white stick of the church at Old Fort Nelson; an irregularity in the endless monotony of forest and river.

A grin of great pleasure creased the sweat and grime of Stanley's face.

'Well, we've done it. And now for a big black steaming steak, a hunk of fresh bread and an ice-cold beer or two or three. And then a long sleep in cool white sheets.' He glanced at me sideways and added, 'Perhaps even a bath when I wake up to remove the upper layers of Duckhams grease.'

It was twilight and two specks of light gleamed from the bank opposite the church. Having no champagne nor even medicinal brandy to celebrate with we fired flares high into the sky. Shimmering pools of green and red and ghostly white appeared in the water as the flares wafted slowly down attached to their little parachutes.

Ginnie was sitting in the sand, a halo of mosquitoes cavorting around her silhouette in the light of the Land-Rover headlights. She had been waiting all day.

* * *

The BBC team were away to the west with the firefighters, filming the greatest fire the local people had ever experienced. They would not be back for a while and we would spend a few days in Fort Nelson repairing the equipment and preparing new stores for the next, more difficult, journey that lay ahead. Stanley and the Scotsmen moved into the doctor's house where Ginnie had been staying.

The doctor had taken his car with him so his garage, amply built to house an American monster, was now overflowing with a mass of expedition equipment.

Ginnie drove me west along the Alaska Highway beyond the sprawling houses of Fort Nelson to an unobtrusive dirt track that led into a forest of ponderosa. At the end of the track was a low log cabin, lent us by Bob Angus, Fort Nelson's news editor. Chickens scuttered in the dirt, and a black shaggy dog, big as a young pony, barked at us from the doorway as though it owned the place. But it responded joyfully enough to Ginnie's voice.

We went in through a double mosquito door and a narrow porch. Inside was everything you have ever dreamed about; the ultimate frontier cabin where comfort is a huge log fire in a wide stone fireplace, beautifully soft bear rugs and sheepskins spread over the floor and low leather-padded armchairs scattered in friendly disarray about the spacious living-room. A well-planned kitchen was partially screened from the living-room and an opening behind the fireplace led to a bedroom and bathroom.

Snowshoes and stuffed mountain goat trophies hung over the fireplace and all manner of carefully chosen objects lined the walls. Beside the doorway stood an instrument which looked much like an unusual piano but in fact played a variety of tin records which were stacked in a cabinet beside the machine. The music was Western country style from several decades back and blended well with the atmosphere of the place.

Ginnie had liked Fort Nelson: the people were kind and genuine. It was a rough community, being after all the most northerly frontier town on that meridian. Its people needed to be tough: in the long winters temperatures stayed far below zero for months on end and in summer heat and humidity, dust, mosquitoes and the fear of fire were ever present, for despite the preparation of a wide forest safety belt around the town, no one was deluded into feeling in any way safe during the months of high fire risk.

Towards the middle of the month the ground baked, and every time Ginnie had driven to the water tower with the radio, she was caked in a powdery dust.

With the dust came the fires and soon the Forest Rangers were seen around town recruiting the first people they could lay hands on as firefighters. Should anyone—white, Indian or Chinaman—refuse the order, he can be clapped straight in jail, for it is a law of the province that every man is liable for firefighting duty, though the unemployed are naturally chosen first, so the majority of fire-fighters are usually Indians.

The worst fire that summer was the Tee fire of Teeter Creek.

On July 24th Ginnie had watched the departure of over forty Indian volunteers to combat the rapidly advancing Tee fire. The men would receive 1.75 dollars an hour, and the group co-ordinators or foremen 2.60 dollars an hour.

For two days the men worked with teams of Caterpillar tractors and bulldozers to clear swathes in the forest. On the third day the blaze swept around behind the 'cats', so they had to leave the area in high gear by way of a creek bed.

Often the fires become so confusing and unpredictable that the firefighters' lives depend entirely upon the helicopters that watch the campaign from above. For the heat waves of an advancing fire move far ahead of it, until the brush is tinder dry. Then, all of a sudden, the undergrowth will reach a flashpoint of heat and ignite far in advance of the main fire. Sometimes, too, burning branches and showers of sparks are blown miles ahead of the conflagration, often over the heads of the firefighters and unbeknown to them. One such spark is sufficient to detonate a heat flashpoint, whereupon an explosion occurs which may burn up the entire length of a tree. This is known as a timber torch or crown candle. Once the fire has reached the ceiling of the forest it spreads with incredible speed from tree to tree. Then, if a circling helicopter is able to spot the danger through the dense pall of smoke, the walkie-talkies of the firefighter foremen crackle with urgency.

Those on the ground, without directions from above, would be in a tricky situation for, in trying to flee one fire, they would as often as not run straight towards another and the secondary fires are often drawn towards the main inferno by the heat vacuum that sucks in air from all around. This same vacuum will cause a man trying to flee before the flames to weaken and then suffocate before he is caught and burnt.

There is usually little to be gained in trying to run from a forest fire for when it crowns with a following wind it can move faster than a galloping horse and water boils in the streams.

Firefighters certainly deserve their high pay, especially the professionals who voluntarily spend the summer months moving from fire to fire.

When a village or, as in the case of the Tee fire, a costly microwave tower and a popular resort are threatened, then aeroplanes are called in to drop hundreds of gallons of chemical fire retardant onto the forest. But this is expensive and since most of the north is uninhabited, fires are often left to burn themselves out. By the last week of July over 100,000 acres of forest were burnt and the smoke pall was so large that it covered Fort Nelson, over 200 miles away, with a carpet of ash and a low noxious smog. Despite unrelenting work by the firefighters the blaze spread out of control until 300,000 acres were black and lifeless and thousands of animals were dead. A change of weather finally subdued the fire.

Ginnie and I spent four days in Bob Angus's cabin, waterproofing maps and planning fuel and food replenishment for the three months' journey to come.

At length everything was ready, the boats skilfully repaired and the engines thoroughly overhauled. Richard Robinson had sent a message that he and his team would meet us at Watson Lake in the Yukon on August 8th. (Bryn was not to reappear again for some weeks.) We had come to Fort Nelson on the Alaska Highway and now we were continuing along it towards the Yukon.

*   *   *

The Highway runs for 1,220 miles through Canada and 300 miles through Alaska to Fairbanks. Such was the American panic in 1942 when it was built that the road was completed in only two years. The Japanese never landed but the road served to open up the north and gave access to a land rich in raw materials and some of the finest, wildest scenery in the world.

From December until March the gravel Highway lies beneath a coating of hard-packed snow at temperatures of below sixty degrees Fahrenheit. During the spring the snow melts, creating black-ice conditions followed by a heavy thaw that washes away culverts and often renders the route unusable.

In summer the problem is dust which causes appalling car crashes. Sixty-foot container lorries roar along the narrow road and are quite impossible to pass in safety. After a few hours in a choking cloud of red dust behind one of these lorries, many car drivers become suicidally impatient. There was more than met the eye, we decided, to the brightly coloured signs on the rear window of every other vehicle that passed us proclaiming 'Alaska or Bust'.

Two hundred miles from Fort Nelson we came to a turquoise lake set deep among jagged mountains of red Torridonian sandstone. Clusters of chalets with a fringe of neatly mown lawns nestled by the lakeshore and the large wooden sign over a corral gate said Highland Glen.

Ginnie had an introduction to the owner of the place. He was a Scotsman, and, noting that we were emissaries of Scotland's only cavalry regiment, he announced free food, drink and accommodation for all.

As a small token of thanks we gave him one of our Black and White whisky bottles and followed him to the laird's lair, a magnificent room with high stone walls liberally studded with highland souvenirs, dirks, horns and even a hefty claymore.

Should we ever write of our travels, said our host, we were on no account to mention his name. Once this was agreed he launched into a long description of his youth in a feudal castle in the Highlands. His father had become impoverished, he said, through giving so much to the poor of his parish and he had come to Canada as a young man to avoid the snobbery of the other lairds.

We were most interested, if somewhat bewildered, by his early history, as Ginnie and I had lived for some time but a few miles from the castle of his memories. He showed us a flood channel not far from his little estate where the gravel spoil of a wide alluvial fan led down from the mountains, and into the lake.

'It'll be our ruin one day,' he said with a grin. 'Every spring, when the snows melt somewhere up in those mountains, a lake is

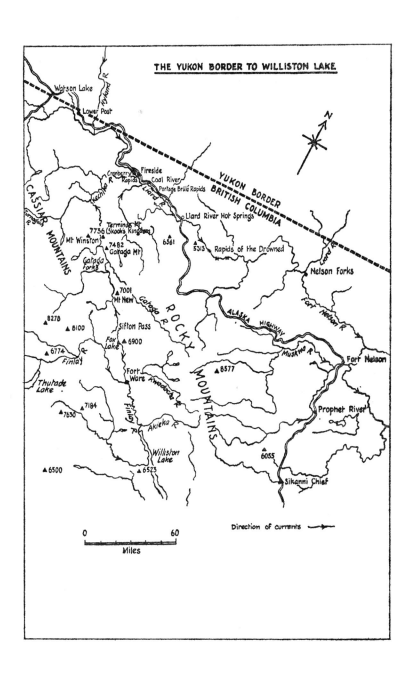

THE YUKON BORDER TO WILLISTON LAKE

Watson Lake

Lower Post

Nyland R.

CASSIAR MOUNTAINS

Turnagan R.

Kechika R.

Cranberry Rapids
Fireside
Coal River
Portage Brûlé Rapids

YUKON BORDER
BRITISH COLUMBIA

Liard R.

Liard River Hot Springs

6561

5315 Rapids of the Drowned

Nelson Forks

Liard R.

Fort Nelson R.

Terminus Mt
7736 (Skooks Kingdom)

Mt Winston
7482 Gataga Mt

Gataga Forks

7001
Mt New

Gataga R.

ROCKY

8278

8100

Sifton Pass

6774
Finlay R.

Fox Lake
6900

Fort Ware

Thutade Lake

7184

7630

Akiaka R.

Finlay R.

Williston Lake

6500

6523

MOUNTAINS

ALASKA HIGHWAY

Muskwa R.

Fort Nelson

8577

Prophet River

6055

Sikanni Chief

N

0   60
Miles

Direction of currents →

formed and its outlet choked by iceblocks. When the water level reaches a certain height, the pressure bursts the ice plug and a deluge of water, iceblocks, and boulders roars down the valley and into the lake. As you can see, it's always missed us by a couple of hundred yards so far, but one year, who knows?'

Our host showed us the fossilised ribs, vertebrae and teeth of mastodons he had found in the mountains around the lake and also the best areas for rare plants which we collected carefully and prepared in the press lent by the Royal Botanical Gardens of Kew.

We left the glen and its kindly but eccentric owner and soon passed the blackened slopes of the Liard Hot Springs. Still smouldering devastation stretched from horizon to horizon.

The Highway passes over a friendly stream called the Hyland River.

Just five miles north of the road, this river crosses from the Yukon into British Columbia so we made camp in a clearing and, leaving the soldiers to prepare the boats, drove west along the Highway to Watson Lake in the Yukon, self-styled gateway to Alaska. Here we located a ton and a half of BP fuel drums at a freight depot and somehow managed to load them onto the Land-Rover and trailer.

The Duty Mountie at Watson Lake made a note to listen for our radio signals every evening for the next two months and the local Forest Ranger warned us that a large fire was presently burning on both banks of the Kechika River somewhere around Scoop Lake. The fire hazard was extreme he said owing to the high humidity factor and we would do well to keep our eyes open when moving through the bush of the Rocky Mountain Trench.

The Ranger was a small efficient man and keen to help. He said that he had often flown along the Trench spotting fires and the only trails he'd ever seen anywhere in the valleys were the narrow game trails of moose and bears which headed off in every direction. He had heard of the occasional trapper taking his boat up the Kechika as far as Gataga Forks which was 115 miles south of the Alaska Highway at Fireside. But from Fireside, he reminded us, there were 200 miles of nothingness until we were over the Pass and down to Fort Ware on the Tochieka or Fox River. So once we had reached Gataga Forks we would have to cut our way through the bush. What would we do with our boats then? he wondered.

I explained that, fearing a long portage, we had brought portable canoes with us. We would stow these in the rubber boats, and if we could indeed navigate no further than these Forks of which he talked, then some of us would take the boats back to Fireside whilst the rest waited at the Forks with the kit and canoes. Ginnie would then have to drive the boats on the vehicles from Fireside round by way of the Alaska Highway and dirt roads to Fort Ware or as near it as possible. The boat crews would have to be brought back to the canoe camp at the Forks by a small seaplane. Then we would all continue south up the Upper Kechika to its headwaters, portage over the Pass with everything on our backs and canoe down the Tochieka River to Fort Ware.

I was thinking aloud but the Ranger seemed to consider my impromptu plan reasonable enough. He didn't know whether a seaplane could land at Gataga Forks but suggested we see Jim Close of Watson Lake Flying Services. If anyone could land us where we wanted to go in the north, he would.

We found Jim Close by his lakeside office in oily dungarees tinkering with the engine of a Beaver floatplane. Other seaplanes, mostly small Cessnas, bobbed beside the low jetty and soon Stanley Bridcutt, Jim's elder partner, arrived and listened to our problem.

After much discussion, it was agreed that he would drop off fuel drums for us at a place called Moose Licks along the Kechika, and that, if required, he would be able to land quite close to Gataga Forks. This he would do for a reduced fee in return for mentions of his company wherever possible.

And so, knowing very little about the country which lay ahead, seven men in three rubber boats entered the Hyland River at midday on August 9th and followed the swift current south from the Yukon into British Columbia. Fifteen hundred miles to the south, as the rivers ran, the Fraser empties into the Pacific by the 49th Parallel.

7

The Kingdom of Skook

THE HYLAND WANDERS SOUTH THROUGH FORESTED HILLS. NOT SO
many years ago an old-timer named Bill Zenchesen had panned for
gold where the crystal-clear Hyland meets the wide Liard in low
marshland. He worked his claim for many months and made his
fortune; every yard of gravel yielded ten dollars of gold. His friend
Bill English was not so lucky: for thirty years he wandered along
panning the streams. His spoils paid for his grub but he never found
a mother lode. It is true gold-fever country, north of the Rockies and
south of the Klondike.

Soon we left the Hyland River and joined the Liard flowing east.
The weather smiled on us and we were averaging eighty miles a day
until we came to the Cranberry Rapids above Fireside. Their roar
was audible from afar and we camped a mile upstream between
the river and the Highway for the two run close and parallel at this
point.

The forest is dense by the Liard but there are hidden bits of
history if you know where to look along the western bank. There is a
place called Alan's Lookout where once this wily robber thieved
from fur trappers. His erstwhile haunt is high above the Liard and
overlooks a single rounded boulder in the river. In the deep wood
immediately behind the boulder, not twenty yards back from the
highwater mark, lies a gold mine. Here we found the little cabins of
the six Chinamen who once, over forty years ago, cleared an area of

two acres by hand and pickaxe. From a spring a mile above their open mine, they dug a water channel which, by gravity, gave them running water to wash the gold from the gravel. Every inch of ground had been turned, every boulder split: they had even dug horizontal shafts into the hillside. These had long since caved in, but the shored-up mouths were still visible.

We had been told of the mine and the miners' fate by a man from Fireside. The six miners had collected a fortune in gold (a million dollars is a conservative estimate of their takings), loaded their riverboat and set off down the Liard. They sank in the Cranberry Rapids, their boat was later found empty, and every man was drowned.

Then in 1968 two Russians, expert slalom canoeists, set out to navigate the Liard from source to mouth. One drowned in the Cranberry Rapids and the other was fished out a few miles downstream, just above the Rapids of the Drowned and the more terrible Portage Brûlé Rapids.

Some distance below the gold mine we ran ashore on smooth white sand and walked into the forest. It was a while before our eyes grew accustomed to the shade and we saw the cabin, skilfully built and sturdy like the food cache behind it.

Inside, Stanley lit a match and spiders scurried along their dusty webs thick with desiccated hornets, wasps and smaller spiders. A sweet, musty smell hung heavy in the single low room. Axes, loops of wire snares and moose antlers hung from nails. Old advertising posters of the Hudson's Bay Company were plastered cockeyed on the walls. I disliked the place for no identifiable reason.

Dancing Charlie had lived and died here: he was buried thirty years or so ago beside the creek and, in Watson Lake, they still tell of the pre-war days when Charlie came to town with his furs. He was lonely and drank his hard-earned money away in a very short while but always, before succumbing to Bacchic oblivion, he would dance. If there were no barmaids, squaws, nor even a long-suffering fellow trapper in view, then Charlie would dance by himself. Since his death no one had come to the cabin for few knew where it was and boats are hard to come by on the Liard. No one except Yukon

Joe, a wild drunk Indian who shot up a saloon, thieved and raped both sides of the border and escaped into thin air from the Mounties. When winter came and the Liard froze, Yukon Joe left the haven of Dancing Charlie's cabin and was living it up in the warmer climes of Prince George when the Mounties finally caught up with him.

We left the cabin and returned to the sandy beach for a meal and some Liard water which tasted unpleasant, worse even than the Nahanni. It was less muddy but heavily impregnated with lime. We packed our waterproof bags and fitted oars to the boats.

The Cranberry Rapids promised to be interesting so Ben ferried the BBC to the far bank. The river is 600 yards across or more and the rapids are a mile long so there are many possible routes to choose between. There were also, it seemed to me watching through binoculars from the Highway, many impossible routes. Otherwise why did the Chinese drown here and the Russian canoeist? Perhaps others too, for the people of Fireside, a mile down the Highway, said no one but the second Russian had ever survived the cataract.

The Scotsmen were unperturbed. They openly proclaimed their little C-Craft *Oor Wee Darlin'* to be superior to the heavier RFDs; certainly it was faster. They decided on a very different route from that which Stanley and I considered the safest. Also they would have nothing to do with oars, believing paddle-power to be far more effective.

The entire length of the rapids was strewn with rock slabs against which the water dashed in confusing turmoil descending a series of chutes that I thought might prove our undoing.

Stanley however seemed quite sure we would make it and looked almost happy as we cast off from the bank. He checked that the outboard was working and then locked it in the horizontal position, its shaft high and dry. There were too many surface rocks to chance using the motors, which would be dangerous anyway if we capsized. If this happened we both knew the drill—hold onto the boat whatever happens. Otherwise you are sucked down below the chutes and toyed with for a long while in the hydraulic waves, the great curling breakers which mark time below each chute.

We had not used oars before in rough water and were surprised how effective they proved in all but the most powerful currents. There are three oars and both crewmen must pull as one for the system to work. Once in the grip of a chute or a whirlpool they were useless, and at no time could they be used for motivation. For steerage however, in or out of the rough stuff, they were usually sufficient to keep the bows facing the oncoming waves.

As we neared the upper rim of the first chute we could see nothing. The noise was frightening. My lips were dry. I sat squarely on a fuel drum clutching both oars and facing the direction of travel. This was not of course the orthodox method of rowing, but then these were not orthodox rowboat conditions. Oarsmen traditionally face the stern and have to squint over their shoulder to check their course.

I was rowing hard upstream whilst the boat raced down stream — which struck me at the time as being more or less what I had been doing much of my life.

I glanced back at Stanley: he was kneeling in the stern wedged up against the transom, and the veins of his forehead stood out beneath his orange crash helmet as he strained against the rudder oar.

A wave crashed over the side tubing, slamming against Stanley. He was small but very strong and, ignoring the temporary immersion, pulled his oar powerfully to the starboard. The boat responded and a squat black rock blurred past to the left.

Now we were rising and falling and wheeling, even moving backwards. Sometimes we hit rock and the whole craft tilted dangerously. An oarblade split but the remnant seemed effective. I realised that I had lost my mental picture of the rapids' geography. There was no time to worry, only to pull harder, to fight the rearing bows and keep the wave crests to our front.

Perhaps Stanley had remembered our planned route. At any rate we came through to the central shelf of the cataract and spotted Paul on the bank crouched over his tripod.

His position we knew was directly above the steepest chute. Ahead of us and straight across from Paul a long black reef split the river. To its right was a sinkhole which had looked quite impassable through binoculars; I knew nothing of the river's nature to the left of the reef but it could hardly be worse.

H   113

At first the reef seemed too close to do anything except keep a steady course but, when a contrary current sideslipped our boat to port, spinning us violently, we seized our chance and pulled like galley slaves to gain the far side of the rocks.

The great reef was almost upon us: Stanley yelled something but his voice was lost in the pounding of water on rock. Then we were in the heart of the cataract, the boat totally submerged and we two clinging to the safety lines with shoulders stooped against the weight of water that swept over us.

The whole craft shuddered. For a moment we were static. I opened my eyes—we were still in the boat and clear of the reef but the hull was jammed on a rock and the river flowed over us. We dared not let go of the lines, for we should be swept away to the lower reefs.

Luck was with us: the hydraulic below the reef snaked towards us as though to crush us finally. Its power shifted the boat and we were free. Cartwheeling out of control, we limped to the bank beyond the final reefs with two of the hull tubes punctured.

Since Richard, Paul and Ben were filming, Corporal Wallace brought their boat through the rapids. For a long while, the black boat rotated above the central reef, trapped in an eddy which resisted every effort of the crew to row clear. Seven times it circled helplessly and then, through a whim of the current it shot free. It passed well to the side of the central reef, disappeared for a while and came clear of the hydraulics moving backwards.

Then the C-Craft appeared in the upper rapids. It seemed to be thrown about a great deal more than the larger boats and the Scotsmen worked like demons with their short paddles. Most of the time they were lost from sight in the wave troughs.

They came through the upper chutes and began the steep run to the central reef. They made no attempt to traverse left. I gesticulated wildly; shouting a warning. Then it was too late; they were in the grip of the right-hand channel; a sheer ten-foot drop to the sinkhole.

The river seemed to swallow them up. I saw the boat stand upon its end as it slammed into the hydraulic maelstrom below the fall.

One of the crew, thrown clear, was instantly sucked out of sight. The other man and the craft itself was hidden by the waves. I noticed Stanley tugging at the starter cord in the damaged RFD. The BBC team were filming the sinkhole. I thought, 'Thank God the C-Craft's engine isn't running.'

A paddle raced away from the sinkhole in the current and the C-Craft, upside down now, followed soon after with one of the crew clining to the outer safety line. Then a head popped up close by and everything was whisked away in a welter of foam to the rocks below.

Stanley came upon both men lying across the boat's keel a mile below the rapids. They were badly shaken but Joe soon recovered, and Jack, though shaking and white, was busy chatting up a pretty young Canadian girl by the time I arrived with the BBC team.

The Cranberry Rapids were behind us and I felt relieved. It was not for many days that I learnt how badly Jack's morale had been affected by the capsize.

He had been frightened when, ejected from the boat, there was nothing firm to hold on to and, under water, he lost all sense of direction. Despite his lifejacket, the undercurrents had pulled him deep turning him over and over and battering him against submerged rocks. He had hurt the back of his head despite his helmet and was quite dazed when he came to the surface. Reaction set in slowly but surely. He grew to hate the roar of rough water ahead and came out in a cold sweat whenever we talked of the great Fraser Rapids to the south.

It rained hard for two days and we waited whilst the rubber solution hardened over the long rents in the old RFD's tubing. Whilst we waited we planned our strategy up the Kechika, deciding to take Corporal Wallace and Ginnie with us so that they could help crew the rubber boats back to Fireside from Gataga Forks. With two extra people and 200 gallons of fuel we were going to be heavily laden indeed.

The Kechika or Big Muddy River seems wilfully to discourage visitors for its most violent rapids run near to its mouth and recur in fitful rashes for twenty miles. It must be one of the least frequented rivers in the world as a result. Even the Indians leave it alone. A single white man lives about halfway along its length, running a centre for big-game hunters. He is called Skook Davidson and Skookum is Indian for *the tough one*. All Skook's hunters, guides, and provisions are flown in by floatplane to his ranch beneath 6,000-foot-high Terminus Mountain. The Kechika flows due north for the whole of its length. As we would be entering it from its mouth on the Liard River (the Kechika is one of the many tributaries of the Liard, the fourth one we had been on) we would be struggling against its flow all the way.

The first 100 miles upstream to the foot of Terminus Mountain was through a magnificent valley but before we could enjoy the scenery we had to struggle through a mile of such turbulent water that the overladen C-Craft immediately required a tow. After a dozen miles a ridge of rock stretched right across the river, causing much confusion where the water ran back on itself. There were no high waves nor whirlpools but the conflicting currents sucked over the uneven ledge in many directions. It was a dangerous spot. The C-Craft and the black boat were thrown together helplessly, and the smaller craft began to fill with water. A tow was impossible in such conditions so the crew lined her through the obstacle with long nylon ropes.

By dusk we were no more than eighteen miles from the river mouth. Each motor had drunk more than a gallon a mile and my fuel estimates were dangerously wrong. The people of Fireside, especially the Highway Inspector—who himself had lost a riverboat by the mouth of the Kechika and nearly drowned—had said the current would flow at three knots. Its speed I estimated was at least six knots in strength which meant we would run out of petrol some forty miles short of Terminus Mountain—despite the fuel cache arranged at Moose Licks.

It was said that the current slowed down upstream of the Moose Licks, so things might still work out.

We slept by the river. After the evening stew, Joe had spotted a young moose half a mile along the bank taking its evening drink. Grabbing his shotgun and ball-shot cartridge belt, he disappeared into the trees as noiselessly as the thick carpet of dry twigs would allow.

The moose was plainly silhouetted. Suddenly it stood erect listening, then moved into the water and swam strongly to the far bank where it disappeared. Many minutes later, Joe could be seen slinking Indian fashion from the trees. He looked up gingerly from the twigs, gazed around him in growing perplexity and spent the rest of the evening suffering from uninterrupted ribbing by the others.

'And why,' enquired Jack, 'did the Last o' the Mohicans no swim across the burn wi' his gun between his molars? Just think on a' that beautiful meat. And yuh a butcher too! Yuh'd be the last o' the Skibinskis if your kids had to depend on their Dad for their dinner.'

All the way to Moose Licks the river ran demented, but we made good steady progress against the current. When we got there we were delighted to see eight fuel drums, lined up in a neat row, looking forlorn and quite out of place.

After tea and hardtack biscuits, we continued for five miles. There was no rough water now but the current ran as fast as ever and I knew we would eventually run out of fuel unless something was done soon. So we stopped and put all kit that was not vital into the C-Craft, together with the empty fuel drums. All but ten gallons of our total fuel supply was shared between the two larger boats. Jack McConnell, Ginnie and Corporal Wallace climbed aboard the cargo of empty barrels and, much disappointed, disappeared downstream.

We were six in two boats now and went no faster than before but the extra fuel should take us to Skook's cabin if the river speed stayed the same.

For two days we were slowed by thunderstorms when the rain fell vertically, lashing the river and soaking us to the bone. In the high Cassiar Mountains which lay to our right in the west we could see white patches among the peaks though it was still only mid-August. Some of these were small hanging glaciers which remain in the high peaks throughout the year.

I wore three thick sweaters beneath my anorak. We tried to keep warm by singing and swinging our arms about but the tiny stern compartments were too cramped to allow much exercise so the long hours passed and we edged along interminable bends and cursed the wilderness which no longer seemed beautiful.

At night, I would sleep with my damp clothes in the sleeping-bag if it rained or, if it didn't, leave them over a drying line beside our fire. The sleeping-bag began to smell unpleasant—a sort of rotting lichen and cooking fat smell—but it took my mind off the cold through its very nastiness. It is perhaps on these lines that the Arab's universal cure for pain is based. The *wusum* or red-hot iron is applied to the flesh somewhere away from the original pain, and the resulting agony effectually eclipses the earlier discomfort. Sound Muslim logic which doubtless discourages malingerers.

On the morning of the fourth day Terminus Mountain was visible to the south in a blue haze. We had camped above the mouth of the Turnagain River which the Indians call the 'Little Muddy'. In fact it is a river of an unbelievable blue; sometimes azure, often turquoise, which flows into the Kechika by the site of Chee House. The Turnagain traces the erstwhile route of a great ice tongue that once flowed into the Trench from the Cassiars.

Two hundred years ago an Indian trading camp stood where the two rivers meet and the tribes came to Chee House from every direction along the forest trails bringing furs and dried meat for barter. In 1887 a friendly trader named Sylvester established a store here. His interest had been stimulated by the discovery of placer gold on nearby Dease Lake in 1873 which brought a number of miners and prospectors to the Kechika basin. Sylvester built two more stores, connecting the river routes with Chee House, one which he called 'Upper Post' at Mac Dane in the Cassiars and the 'Lower Post' on the Liard which has kept its name.

Now there is no sign of habitation except a mound or two, for the Indians left no artefacts and all but a few have long since been wiped out by disease and starvation. These Indians were always nomadic mountain men, in summer they moved west to catch salmon on the Pacific side of the Rockies, braving the anger of the other Indians in the coastal hills and in winter they moved east to trap the low game country which was mainly inhabited by the indigenous Cree and

Beaver tribes. So life for these Rocky Mountain Cassiar nomads had never been easy. They belonged to a branch of the Athapaskan tribe and were known as Sikanees (Sekani means dwellers of the rocks). The mountain goats provided them with blankets which, when sewn together, would cover the entire family, and skin coats which were worn with the hair inside in the winter and outside in the summer. Often they were forced to live off roots or starve. Many gruesome tales were told by trappers who found skeletons, some still clad in decomposed flesh, propped up in bushes, caves or hollow trees but all such corpses could safely be ascribed to the Sikanees' burial habits. An Indian of any importance would, after death, be placed in a coarse shroud of branches and stood erect against a tree or other convenient prop.

The first whites grew fond of the nomadic Sikanees for they were inoffensive and trustworthy. There were instances of Hudson's Bay Company factors leaving their stores for a month in the winter and returning to find dead Sikanee families, emaciated by starvation, lying in their teepees round the company store. They had known perfectly well that boxes of dried fish were inside the store but to steal would have been unthinkable, so they had waited for the storekeeper's return.

Beyond the Turnagain tributary, the Kechika River slowed down for a while and the boats made better progress, arriving towards midday in a region of utter desolation. The banks were low so that the very size of the disaster was stunning. As far as the eye could see the land rolled black and silent. The endless ranks of pines stood like charred victims of an atomic holocaust. Isolated pines still smoked above us on the banks. Even the birds were gone, save a few high-soaring specks that dropped like stones from time to time; the sharp-eyed birds of carrion. The strength of the grizzly, the speed of the cougar, the camouflage of a million tiny field mice, even the brains of the lonely trapper—nothing is proof against the racing fires of the north.

We met three hunters in two long riverboats, Len Eklund and the de Valereroa brothers. The brothers smelled of beer and one was amiably drunk. They gave us a can of petrol, a shoulder of goat meat, and a crate of beer. They were the only white hunters in the whole of the Northern Trench outside of Skook Davidson's set-up and it seemed they'd been successful for Len Eklund showed us the 40-inch horns of a mountain ram.

They had been a few miles beyond Gataga Forks but their boats were powered by 65-horse-power jets which could operate in much shallower water than our propeller-driven motors. None of them could advise us on the country to the south nor did they think that the old Indian trails to the Pass were still usable. They were leaving now for winter was coming and they had seen the first snow settle in the high Rockies earlier that week.

There followed thirty miles of islands, snyes and shallows but before dusk the slopes of Terminus Mountain lay over our left shoulder and we moored in a narrow creek. The country had changed greatly over the last few miles. For the first time we noticed groves of aspen with much wild thyme and juniper.

This was the Kingdom of Skook and we followed a well-defined trail through the bush with sapling fencing lining both sides of the track. There was a great deal of horse manure and a confusion of hoofprints in the dust. I remembered that Skook was said to own at least 200 pack-horses which he had bred for work with his hunting parties.

We walked uphill for a mile or so between fencing, passing beneath an old sign saying 'Diamond J Ranch — No Shooting on This Land'. Then the trail crossed a creek by a weird Heath Robinson contraption — you could scarcely call it a bridge. Beyond the creek a family of little cabins straddled a clearing high enough above the river to gain a view as wild and panoramic as any king might wish.

Skook was in his bed in the first cabin, an old gnarled man, who peered at me in the gloom. He rose with his hand on his hip where the arthritis pained him and fumbled for a candle to light. 'Well sit down, darn you,' he barked. 'You folk from the old country never seem to know what the Lord gave you asses for.' The candle light flickered along a row of medals nailed to a log. Skook had done a stint in the trenches as a sniper of the 29th Vancouver Battalion during the First World War.

'When it was dark, I used a knife. I remember the time we were guides on night patrol to a British unit—they were greener than grass—I brought their officer back a Jerry's head one night; still scowling it was ... Officer fainted.' Skook chuckled merrily at the memory.

He was not married though he had on many occasions chased squaws up trees, or so he would have us believe. His affection was lavished on his many horses although he could no longer ride and most days he would travel down the ranch trails in an old cart, escorted by an Indian and a flurry of yapping huskies.

There was a region of rolling fields above the cabins, all fenced in and known as the Skookum Freeway for here his horse herds roamed at will except when required to pack supplies to the outlying hunting camps of Broken Bit and Mayfield Lake. When the horses grew too old to work, Skook would let them enjoy their pensions in the meadows 'until the winter finally gets them'.

The winter temperatures were often minus sixty degrees Fahrenheit but Skook's land, all 50,000 square miles of it, lay in a localised semi-arid climate so the snow was lighter than elsewhere which allowed all but the most aged horses to winter in the open with locally cropped swamp grass for hay. Here and there about the trails lay the sun-bleached skeletons of long-dead horses. Skook remembered many of them by name, muttering in nostalgia about the particular foibles of Daisy or Bess as he showed us some scattered bones.

Stopping the cart with a light touch of the reins and a gruff 'Whoa there, damn you,' he pointed across to the great peaks in the south. 'I named that one Mount Winston—over seven and a half thousand feet it is and that tall one over there—higher'n ten thousand feet—I called Churchill's Peak. That's what they're called on the map now but dammit if some darned fool didn't name one of the others after Stalin. I knew Sir Winston, you know... Had a whisky with him during the Gallipoli campaign.'

Skook was over eighty. He had first settled in the Valley in 1939 and started his hunting business from scratch. Now he looked after twenty hunters a year for three weeks each. They were mostly Americans who paid him 150 dollars a day: Skook's guides saw that they were always satisfied and had a shot at their desired trophy even if they didn't bag it.

Just about everyone in British Columbia had heard of Skook: he was a living legend, having once been the finest horseman in the land with many rodeo awards to his credit. On discovering that Joe was Scottish, he announced that he too was from north of the border.

'We lived in Aberdeen and at school we spent a good deal of time praying to the Lord. Right in front of me there was a little gal with a very long pigtail. One Christmas when I was twelve my Dad gave me a lovely knife and I tested it at the very first chance – which was the next time we had prayers. Why, that little gal's pigtail came off at the first slice. That was a beautiful knife but what a fuss there was. Dad felt I would be better off in the colonies and packed me off to BC with ten dollars in my pocket. They do say there are parts of Scotland just like here but I doubt it. I reckon this here's the finest land in the world.'

Skook let us sleep in the hunters' bunkhouse and eat with his household – an Indian, a young lad named Smokey, a visiting Irish doctor, and the cook who was an ex-hippy divorcée called Fern. Her cooking was quite the best thing I had experienced during the expedition; cookies, doughnuts and cakes of every description, salads, moose steaks, and mincemeat all washed down with coffee from a bottomless urn.

We slept well in the warmth of the bunkhouses and left early for the Forks of Gataga, fifteen miles to the south. The going was fast and the countryside very beautiful for the Rockies swept down from the east and the higher Cassiars from the west.

The Gataga River flowed in grey with glacial silt and discoloured the Kechika. The former was more deserving of the name Big Muddy since, immediately above the Forks, the Kechika flowed a lucid blue so that the sandbars were easy to see. But they were impossible to avoid as the river was now too shallow for the long drive-shaft of our motors. We therefore established a camp on the sandy spit between the two rivers and, with the boats empty of kit, returned to Skook's.

Leaving Joe and the camera team with Skook, Stanley and I took the two inflatables back north down the Kechika to Fireside, a journey which, with the current, lasted less than a day. There we met up with Ginnie, Corporal Wallace, Jack McConnell and the C-Craft. Carefully we deflated all three boats and loaded them aboard the vehicles for they were to go by road to Mackenzie, a recently established logging town 400 miles to the south. In Mackenzie Ginnie would have to find a riverboat large enough to carry the three inflatables up Williston Lake and the Finlay River to Fort Ware, a distance of some 350 miles. Before she set off with the boats, Ginnie drove us to Watson Lake Air Services.

A flamboyant young pilot named Bob Mitchell landed the Beaver at Gataga Forks in a driving wind. I watched fascinated as the wings sideslipped and shuddered violently in powerful gusts and down-draughts. We came in fast and bounced along the river, Bob looking anxiously for small snags which might buckle the paper-thin floats. They support two and a half tons at the moment of impact, being handmade and more expensive than the aeroplane itself.

A second quick trip to Skook's and back brought us Joe Skibinski. Then Bob flew the BBC team south to Fox Lake to await our arrival overland. They were to wait for a very long time for no one could tell what trails were available if any, through the ninety-odd miles of forest between Gataga Forks and Fox Lake.

At Fireside only one man, a fur trapper, had travelled over the Sifton Pass. That had been over twenty years ago with Skook and a group of surveyors. He had told me that if Skook himself could not advise us, then no one could.

Skook had been very helpful and full of advice for he considered the trail as very much his own. He had earned his nickname as 'the tough one' it was said through backpacking heavy loads over the Sifton Pass. In the thirties he had made trips to Fort Ware and back solely to collect his mail, liquor and tobacco. Skook's kingdom lies at the northernmost limit of the Rocky Mountain Trench for although the Cassiars continue towards the Yukon, the Rockies lose their identity after Terminus Mountain and dwindle thereafter to low wooded hills owing to a prehistoric lack of Tertiary elevation of the landmass beyond this point. To the south the Trench continues for a thousand miles running south-south-east to Flathead Lake in Montana, USA. Geologists are still uncertain as to the origin of the great intermontane gash which varies from two to ten miles in width with an uneven flow of glacial gravel and detritus which is hundreds of feet in depth. Numerous circular lakes remain where the retreating glaciers were isolated and finally melted.

The Sifton Pass and the Trench had scarcely been used as a through route even in the days of the Yukon gold rush for there were quicker ways to the Klondike by ship to Skagway Inlet, along the Alaskan Panhandle and thence overland. But a few people had tried it in desperation, for the goldrush was a frantic scramble into which many people hurled themselves without much thought. It had all begun in 1896 when a professional prospector named Robert Henderson who had spent his life searching for gold in Australia and America finally struck a modest lode in the Klondike. He told his good news to the first man he met, Carmack, who subsequently made a fortune at Henderson's Bonanza Creek. Poor Henderson's own claim proved worthless and he later died without a penny although the Klondike itself ultimately produced over a hundred and fifty million pounds of gold.

Carmack spread the good news and the following spring many of the lucky 'sourdoughs', so called because they baked their bread with fermented dough rather than yeast, had already returned to San Francisco loaded with gold. The news spread like wildfire not only around the depressed areas of America but all over the world.

Soon men were flocking to the Klondike. Some went by the White Pass over which stores were carried on dogs and horses. The trail was a morass of mud and corpses during the summer, a heaving line of black specks during the bitter winter. People succumbed by the hundreds to the cold, fatigue, starvation and disease and the pack animals died in thousands.

The Chilkoot Pass was too steep for animals so everything had to be carried on the back. A thousand people were killed the first winter when a mountain lake burst through an ice barrier and swept over the trail in a single wave. Heavily laden climbers were killed daily in small numbers but the most memorable day was April 3rd, 1898, when an avalanche buried a wide stretch of the trail beneath twenty feet of boulders and snow. Sixty bodies were recovered and a few frostbitten survivors but when the snow melted a few months later, many more bodies were revealed. These were flung over the mountainside by the summer climbers once their valuables had been looted.

It is estimated that one hundred and five thousand optimists set out for the gold fields during the three-year heyday. Only forty thousand got there, of whom about eight hundred made worthwhile fortunes.

How many aspiring Klondikers travelled and died along the Kechika is not related but in 1898 sufficient governmental interest was aroused in its potentials as a main route to the Yukon for a patrol to be mounted by the North West Mounted Police under one Inspector Moodie. From Edmonton and Prince George he moved slowly north over the Pass to the Turnagain and then west to Dease Lake country. He used local guides and a force of Mounties to cut an excellent pack trail as he went but within a few years the trail was obliterated by forest growth and was never used. The Inspector named the Pass after Clifford Sifton, the Minister of the Interior, and not till 1934 was it again disturbed—this time by Lamarque and the well-known surveyor Swannell, trail-blazers of a much heralded expedition led by the famous Charles Bedaux who had made his name in the Sahara.

The group included Madame Bedaux, two female aides, a Scottish gamekeeper and a vehicle mechanic, who was to look after the Citroën half-tracks. They also brought strings of pack-horses which carried such necessary stores as Devonshire cream and crates of champagne. Rain and snowstorms in August and September forced Bedaux to abandon the Citroëns somewhere to the north of the Sifton Pass and to continue on horseback. But the horses suffered from hoof rot and were shot. The expedition failed and Bedaux said that he would try again. Perhaps he would have but 1939 found him back in the Sahara on a mission for the Germans. The Allied Forces captured him, and, since he was a naturalised US citizen, he was sent to America where he committed suicide shortly before he could be convicted for treason. He is remembered by many in British Columbia, erroneously, as a German spy who tried to find an invasion route through the north-west.

Skook himself had helped the Indians to cut a narrow forest trail from Fort Ware to Lower Post which he had called the Davie Trail in honour of the Indian Chief Davie. Skook had also helped the Americans when they completed a detailed survey of the whole area in 1939 while looking for a possible route for a potential Alaska Highway.

Skook remembered his trail as excellent and doubtless it had been over thirty years before. However I found it ominous that surveyor Hugh Pattinson had described the path, only six months after it had been made, as 'requiring much work every season if the trail is to be kept open, due to washouts, rapid growth and windfalls'. But Skook saw no reason why his trail should have deteriorated. He said that he had sent one of his Indian guides, Frank George, through with thirteen pack-horses, all the way to Fort Ware, only a month before. *He* had found the trail OK. But he admitted to knowing of no white man who had been along the trail since his, Skook's, own last journey.

I met Frank George briefly at Skook's and asked him about the trail.

'You'll be all right,' he said, 'so long as you don't follow a game trail by mistake. They're all over the place.'

I asked him how we were to know the real trail from the game trails.

'Why you just do. I been along that way since I was a kid and you just get to know the right way after a while. But you watch out for bears, man. The very last time I came along the trail, just this side of Gataga Forks, a female grizzly came at me fast and I was lucky. Pumped six shots right into her neck from my ·303 and she dropped a few yards away along the trail. Usually they keep away but, if you surprise them on the trail or with their kids, then they get real mean.'

*   *   *

Stan and I began to paddle our canoes against the power of the Kechika. The Scotsmen soon drew ahead of us and Jack shouted back over his shoulder, 'Ye'll nevver get there afore midnight, old men. But nevver mind, we'll keep the stew warm fer you's.'

Even Stanley hadn't the breath to reply. We were cramped by the two heavy rucksacks between our legs and found it difficult to balance the flimsy canoe. My knuckles kept carping against the back of Stanley's head as the paddle slipped through the water.

We tried keeping away from the bank and found ourselves being swept downriver so we moved close to the bank again whereupon we became entangled with branches and snags which was unpleasant and obstructed all progress.

We tried moving through the woods carrying the laden canoe on our shoulders but gave up after ten yards, ending up wading, or swimming when it was too deep, and pulling the canoe behind us a few inches from the bank.

In two hours we had advanced a mile or so and were both extremely cold. The others had not found the going much easier despite their superior strength and we found them camped in low bushes with tea on the boil.

Next day, with the canoes collapsed into four neat bundles and lashed to our rucksacks, we searched the bush for a trail leading south. It would be useless trying to continue on the river until its current slowed down, something we could check from time to time since, on our map, the dotted line of the trail kept within a mile of the river all the way to Fox Lake.

Each of us had selected his own rucksack from the two types available. I had a Bergen which is bulky but tough; the others had all chosen tripak frames which are far lighter but apt to buckle under an abnormally heavy load. And our loads were, through necessity, slightly over 100 pounds—a weight which is quite tolerable for a short distance when walking on a good surface. Every item carried had been decided upon between the four of us and anything not essential to the journey had been discarded, including tents. We had sufficient dehydrated food for eight days but expected to reach Fox Lake in only six; averaging fifteen miles a day.

Skook's friend, the Irish doctor, had been shocked when he'd watched us pack the rucksacks. We had no axes, only light divers' sheathknives with serrated edges. This he later reported with glee to the Vancouver newspapers, adding that whereas the officer had an adequate rucksack, the poor soldiers were forced to take issue packs, an example of imperialistic ignorance and brutality which he had not expected west of Belfast.

There was not one occasion during the rigours of the next three weeks when we ever required an axe. Indeed we hardly ever used the knives, since the only wood which would burn well was dead and could be broken by hand. Furthermore Jack McConnell's tri-pak rucksack caused him no trouble although his load was appreciably heavier than the others.

Throughout the morning, moving laboriously along a narrow forest trail we overbalanced under the weight of the packs whenever we became wedged between trees or entangled with overhead branches. Many trees too had been blown down across the trail which made things awkward. The heat was intense and there was an abundance of flies. Once fallen over it was extremely difficult to get up again without help from two of the others.

After a trying time we came by noon to three log cabins by the mouth of the Frog River. I was following Jack, who for once had stopped calling me an old man. After an hour Stanley arrived: he was not very much larger than his rucksack but stumbled on manfully. He tottered over by the fire we had made at the cabins, his face pale, sickly and wet with perspiration. He winced with a spasm of coughing and spat a gob of deep red blood onto the grass. His groin was paining him badly and he said he had been tasting the salty tang of blood for a long while.

He was our only trained medic, but it seemed obvious that his

Joe and Jack—the paddle-power men . . .

. . . do a spot of unscheduled underwater work . . .

. . . and test the 're-righting' grips of their boat.

Old Skook in his Kingdom—a hundred miles from anywhere.

An Indian cabin on the Frog River.

condition could not be treated lightly. To continue further into the wilderness in his present state would be unwise.

Another hour passed by before Joe Skibinski arrived. He had fallen over a log and wrenched his back so that it pained him to move. He had not mentioned it before but he'd spent several weeks in hospital five years earlier after an injury to his spine when skiing. And now the old pain had come back. At first he had gritted his teeth and hauled his pack along the trail tied to two saplings. This soon proved too awkward owing to the number of fallen trees and Joe had covered the last two miles in considerable pain.

Skook's cabins were some thirty river miles away from us and downstream all the way. Reluctantly it was agreed that Stanley and Joe should return to Skook's by canoe and radio for a plane to take them to Fox Lake where they might rest and recover with the others.

They assembled their canoe and left, wishing us luck.

Jack and I tried to press on that evening but the heat had sapped much of our energy and my head began to feel dizzy as we followed a narrow path that snaked along the rim of a high slope. Then the trail veered to the east away from the river and ahead, where the trail should have run, there was nothing but dense forest as far as the distant horizon where the peaks of the Cassiars fused with the Rockies.

The forest was impenetrable; we tried to move through it, without success. Our water-bottles were empty so we camped above the river beneath a thin sheet of polythene and slept.

8

The High Rockies

W ITH PADDED LIFEJACKETS TO PROTECT OUR BACKS, THE METAL
frames of the rucksacks could not tear at our skin but each time a
boot slid off a rock and sank into the marsh or an overhanging
branch caught hold of the rucksack, we would lose balance and crash
over into the undergrowth to lie quite helplessly like upsidedown
turtles until the other man could slowly manoeuvre himself, without
losing his own balance, and haul away at his fallen partner with
much mutual grunting and groaning.

Once Jack and I both fell over whilst crossing a network of fallen
trees too high to scissor the legs over and too low to crawl beneath.
For a while we lay laughing weakly at the comic side of things but
the situation might well have become anything but funny for it was
sometimes physically impossible to escape from the constricting
shoulder and stomach straps when spreadeagled on one's back
amongst the huge tree trunks and barely able to breathe.

We would halt for five minutes every half-hour, too exhausted to
talk. A few mouthfuls of water, and the painful feeling of blood
returning to shoulders and arms. Then on again: through marsh
and the rotten orange muck which separated many pools of bog
cotton from which mosquitoes and midges rose in humming clouds.

The compass showed our trail to be heading ever further to the
north-east and by noon it was clear something was wrong. We
stopped in a copse of lodgepole pine, high above the swamps and

almost insect-free. Jack started a fire and used our last water making tea. Leaving my pack with him I continued along the trail which ran through a swamp for two miles to a rocky outcrop which I climbed and, for the first time, could see above the forest line.

The map indicated a high ridge running north–south to the east of and parallel with the Kechika. The dotted trail was shown to run between the river and the ridge called the Forsberg Mountain.

There was a wide view from my hillock and no longer any doubt that we had gone wrong. Our trail such as it was ran away from the river and the Trench, leading deep into the Rockies and yet it was the only trail we had seen. There simply had not been any alternative route from the very bank of the Kechika, and our path was, after all, often marked by tree-blazes — where branches, even whole trees, had been lopped off by an axe or saw. And hoofmarks were visible sometimes among the hotchpotch of wolf, bear and moose prints.

I remembered Skook's advice clearly. 'There's only one trail to Ware, dammit, and that runs clear as a bell beside the river. The trees're blazed and old Frank George came through with a dozen horses only weeks back. Why, you can't go wrong, not even if you're an Englishman.'

Well, we had gone wrong and it could only be due to carelessness. Somewhere along the trail we must have taken a wrong turning from the main southerly route. Subconsciously I felt this could not be so since if there *was* only one route we must be on it. But once committed to a trail leading away from the Trench and its rivers, it might lead almost anywhere. Safer to double-check first.

Jack was dismayed at the news. Eight hours of effort wasted, but he shrugged goodnaturedly and we returned the way we had come, reaching the Kechika soon after dusk. Having no water we slept in the bushes a few feet from the river. It was a fine night and there was much coming and going of animals, for three well-used game trails converged close to our sleeping-bags. Not far from our camp, we found a shallow trough in the ground which, by its smell, was definitely a moose wallow. Wallows are made by lone bull moose before the rutting season. Once they have pawed out a suitably sized hole they use it as a lavatory for a while and then roll in it with great pleasure and much noise. Perhaps they hope to win over their favoured cow moose by smelling more beautiful than any other suitor.

Some of the animals that moved about us that night were large enough to shake the ground—perhaps bears, but more probably deer since we had seen a great many deer-spoor along the narrow game 'runs'.

The largest deer are the moose, called Moos-wah by the Indians. They are dangerous if cornered, disturbed with young, or during the rutting months. They have been known to kill bears and wolves with their sharp front hooves and the jagged set of horns that often achieve a six-foot span.

The slightly smaller Wapiti deer or elk weigh up to 800 pounds, and are great fighters for the favours of their females. Usually the larger a Wapiti stag, the more numerous his does. They charge one another at full speed during rutting battles and their long horns sometimes become inextricably interlocked so that both stags subsequently die of starvation, their combined harems becoming a windfall for the first third-party that happens along.

The smaller mule-deer are more numerous but very shy and we saw them only in the distance. They are said to have long scent glands running down the lower part of their rear legs unlike any other known deer.

Later, in the High Rockies, we saw many caribou which came quite close to us but seemed to steer clear of the lower valleys and all but the highest mountain creeks.

In the morning the heavens opened and dark clouds hid the mountains. We shivered by a reluctant fire long enough for our daily ration of four oatmeal biscuits to dissolve in two mugfuls of water and form a glutinous porridge that we laced with salt and drank down with tea. Then we helped one another into the rucksacks and tottered about for a while, cursing the aches and pains of bruised muscle and taut blisters.

For two miserable hours we searched carefully through the dripping foliage and found a great many game trails but not a trace of a blazed route except for the one we had travelled the day before.

Shivering from the cold, and wet to the bone, we discussed our predicament. Already we were a day behind schedule which meant a day's less rations. To force a way through the bush, with our great cumberson packs jamming at every step, was positively the last alternative.

The trail was, despite Skook's advice, quite definitely not where the map showed it to be so the only answer lay in the hope that the blazed trail, for topographical reasons, wound its devious way away from the Trench only to turn back again at some later stage and rejoin the Kechika further south – a detour perhaps which Skook was aware of but had forgotten about.

And so for three long and very wet days we followed the trail through swamps and tall dark forests, winding up steep hills and down slippery inclines. Jack missed his footing during the morning of the second day, falling from the path and disappearing down a gloomy slope between the boles of enormous hemlock trees. When I found him he was badly scratched and bruised. For a while he could not manage his pack and, when we took off his boot, we found the ankle to be badly swollen. We wrapped it in a shell dressing and jammed it back in the boot quickly before it became too swollen to fit.

The forests were dank and foetid; the original Catskill woods, I reflected, upon which Arthur Rackham might well have based his fiendish devil-grottoes wherein evil goblins feed on strange toad-stool mutations and bloodsucking bats roost in the gnarled tentacles of giant pines.

It rained continuously and streams flowed fast along the trail, forming deep pools in basins between the knee-high roots that crisscrossed everywhere.

Jack, determined to press on, limped beneath the heavy pack. We were cold and wet at all times and walked in silence following the dim marks of the trail, a tree-scrape here, a slashed branch there, sometimes a double gash in the bark of a fir, but the most helpful and sure signs of direction were the sawn-off ends of trees that had once lain across the trail.

Often giant lodgepole pines blocked our route so that a way must be forced through the undergrowth to rejoin the trail beyond. At such times it was best to drag the packs behind us bit by bit, it being impossible to move in such country with them on.

We heard the thud of hooves or paws as heavy creatures moved ahead through the trees and twice we saw fresh wolf-spoor cross the trail. That morning, thin slivers of ice had fallen from every branch we pushed past, many wedging between our shoulders and packs until they melted.

At night we slept close together beneath the polythene sheet, by a fire coaxed from old bark and moss from beneath fallen tree trunks.

Every day our dehydrated menu was the same and every meal was the best thing that ever happened — each mouthful savoured with care and reverence.

One morning the trail crossed a wide creek and then recrossed it no less than sixteen times. With the rushing freezing water up to our waists we moved with the utmost care. To slip on the slimy rocks along the riverbed or to yield to the powerful tug of the current would mean a wet sleeping-bag and then our troubles would really begin. But the cold did serve to distract our minds from the misery of bruised shoulders and the chafe of wet trousers against the now raw skin of our crotches. Our feet were painful in the mornings when first we laced wet boots over a mass of squelching blisters. But after an hour or so of trudging, the blisters would stop complaining.

We moved slowly and did not stop to rest for we learnt that, once cold, our bodies would not warm up again unless we built a fire by the creek and stood by it steaming for an hour or so till our clothes dried out. On again, and within five minutes we'd be soaked through, for the foliage was wringing wet.

On the fourth day the trail led deep between mountains. We could see their glistening grey flanks through chinks in the roof of the forest.

We became very hungry but, though we saw many animals, they were off and away before Jack could detach the rifle from my pack. Our morale was greatly boosted when Jack saw a Spruce or

Franklin's grouse watching us with great curiosity. They are known locally as 'fool-hens' and this one lived up to its nickname. It was on a low branch some eight yards away.

Very carefully Jack removed his 9-mm pistol from its holster and carefully took aim at the pretty dappled breast of the bird. He missed but it stayed put nonetheless clucking in indignation. It fixed its would-be executioner with a stony glare, its breast heaving with ire. Perhaps its scrutiny embarrassed Jack, who missed with two further shots. Since we had very little ammunition and I was quite overcome with the thought of delicate grouse meat roasting for supper, I took the pistol and, with the first shot, removed a twig beside the grouse. More clucking and breast twitching. Two more shots and, at last, blinking as though mortally offended, the grouse toppled from its branch and lay still.

We had fishing lines but there were no fish in the creeks. Eight little polythene ration bags were left: enough dehydrated food for four days. Would we break through to the Trench and Fox Lake before our food gave out? I couldn't tell, for map-reading is out of the question when no landmarks are visible, nothing but the undergrowth for twenty yards on either side!

On the evening of the fourth day the trail gave out altogether in a region of many creeks, a thousand wooded valleys, and great looming canyons that enclosed us as though we would wander for ever in this gloomy land.

The gamble had failed. Who had made the trail, or when; or why it stopped in the middle of nowhere, we would never know. But it would obviously not lead us to the Sifton Pass. We must cut off west by compass-bearing to reach the Rocky Mountain Trench again and then, if there were still no track beside the river, we must wade up the Kechika to its headwaters. Any other course would amount to admitting failure.

The greatest worry was that Jack's ankle which pained him greatly now might give out and immobilise him completely.

Every evening we set up the radio with its powerful dipole aerial, to contact the Mounties on 4785 megacycles. We could hear them clearly but never received an answer to our signals.

'Hallo RCMP. Any Station RCMP. This is British Expedition RMT. This is British Expedition RMT. Do you hear me? Radio check. Over.'

Once we heard Victoria calling JD9. That was a thousand miles away but sounded loud and clear. Then Fort Smith called urgently for Fort Chippewan to send an ambulance. Little Tommy Moore — two years old – was seriously ill. At eight o'clock one evening, the hour of our scheduled call to the Watson Lake Mounties, they came up as soon as Jack tuned in but they were preoccupied with a young Indian who'd stolen a car and never answered our oft repeated signals—though our battery reading was strong and steady: the mountains must be blocking our transmission.

So we moved into the undergrowth and upwards, hauling ourselves through the dank and dripping forest, seeming hardly to progress at all. Jack's ankle hurt badly so I took the radio from him. After eight hours' toil we came above the treeline and moved up a steep gully of rubble and thornbush between sheer walls of rock. The wind was biting and lashed through our wet shirts. For three hours we stumbled upwards catching hold of thorn branches when our feet slid on the rubble which clattered away down the mountain threating to take us with it.

Despite the cold I was thirsty but there were no creeks here. We were well above the watershed and from nowhere, as we inched up the highest slopes, the snow came in violent wind-blown scurries. We found a narrow space between two rocks, draughty but protected from the direct sting of the blizzard.

Jack looked pale and lay shivering, nursing his foot.

There was no dead wood, only wet brush, and an hour passed before a fire would light with sufficient heat to boil water and put some life back into us. Certainly we could not stay long at this height. We must move down to water and shelter before dusk but in many places sheer cliffs fell away for thousands of feet; no place for movement in bad visibility.

We were lucky. The snowstorm subsided, a howling wind drove the mist past in long shadowy wreaths so that for moments the country about and far below us was visible. We were on top of the world.

Moving from the warmth of our shelter we stumbled to the edge of the ridge.

The scenery was breathtaking. I clutched my map firmly against the gale and oriented it by the compass. To the south an armada of jagged pinnacles floated black above a sea of cloud. Ahead, to the west, an unbroken line of bald-topped mountains and beyond them, from time to time, a glimpse of the razor ridges of the Cassiars through fleeting mist. To return to the Trench would involve climbing this western range which, by my map, was nowhere under 6,000 feet and in many places well over 8,000 feet.

The great peak to our immediate front was probably Mount New or Bighorn Mountain and we ourselves were on an eastern outcrop shown as being 6,000 feet high. To reach the main range we would have to descend through dense forest, find a way through a confusing series of re-entrant valleys, and then climb again with our meagre supply of rope and artificial climbing aids over the bare rock peaks above the Trench.

Before leaving the summit ridge Jack set up the radio and signalled for half an hour. A policewoman with a husky voice was giving information about a criminal named Merrill but no one answered our call.

A near-vertical valley fell away between the cliffs; its slopes densely forested. We moved down it with great caution for the undergrowth was deep in decayed vegetation and Jack's ankle would not stand another bad fall.

Night found us at the head of a tiny creek with a great fire crackling through branches of wet pine. Should we fail to scale the western ridge, what then?

One mile an hour was speedy progress in these forests. With no trail, there were swamps and muskeg cushions to be crossed, acres of giant deadfall pines to be climbed over, under or around, and worst of all the everlasting tangle of dripping wet whiplash branches to be forced through. At no time were we sure of our route; as we could not see even the nearest mountain nor anything but the immediate tangle of forest. Even the compass was suspect for there are many mineral deposits in such regions.

Mostly we followed creeks with a westerly tendency and wherever possible moved along the narrow game trails which laced the valleys but unfortunately never went very far before petering out.

At dusk each day we would find a level spot near a creek and place a thick network of pine branches over the saturated ground, then our groundsheets, sleeping-bags and single blankets. In the mornings there would be a solid sheet of ice beneath the ground sheet. Perhaps it would have been wise to have taken a tent but we were overladen as it was and the light polythene cover served to keep away the direct impact of rain and hailstorms.

One night our camp was by the edge of a swampy clearing in deep forest and for once the rain had stopped. Momentarily forgetting the cold, I peered out of my sleeping-bag at the unusual sight of a family of flying squirrels playing games. The little animals have layers of slack skin on both sides of their bodies between their limbs so that, aided by long flat tails, they can glide over fifty feet through the air, ending with a sharp upward curve, that brings all four paws into simultaneous contact with their landing place. Five shadows flew from tree to tree: aerial blobs whistling quietly, tracing an erratic route around and across the clearing.

Towards the end of August a day came when we struggled clear of the forest at 5,000 feet, only to find all further progress barred by a sheer wall of rock. We could go no further west: it might take days to find a way around the buttress. To the south lay unknown valleys, the inner Rockies and the great glaciers of the Lloyd George Icefield. There was now no course open to us other than to return to Skook's before our rations gave out, collect a further supply and set out again to force a way along the course of the Kechika itself. But even that would be impossible unless we could quickly get back to our earlier trail through the unbelievable maze of winding inter-locked valleys.

We slept little that night, for the cold was intense. Rising shivering before dawn we found our clothes still damp. It was the worst moment of the day, when we were already cold and hungry, to have to put on wet clothes, frost-hard boots over blistered feet, and finally the heavy rucksacks. Everything protested at once and we hobbled about lamely, wincing as the metal pack frame settled into our backs.

I had two places where the flesh of my shoulders was raw and festering and a rash of swollen boils across the small of my back where the pack rubbed at every step.

And then the sting of branches whipping at face and arms, a thousand slivers of ice scattering down neck and shirt front, and the painful rub of wet trouserleg against freshly bleeding crotch rubbed raw during the preceding days. But what was worst was the nagging thought that an ankle might twist. Jack's caused him much worry being green and badly swollen.

Would we ever find the trail back to Skook's? Would searching aeroplanes find us? After all they would look along the Kechika or within a mile of it at best, and we were many miles away to the east invisible beneath a dark green carpet. We had no Sarbe emergency beacons with us and could only hope that sooner or later someone would hear our radio calls before the batteries ran out.

After seven hours of spongy muskeg we were near the end of our tether. It was not possible to move away from the swamps without leaving our north-easterly compass bearing. But our legs sunk into the squelching mire to our knees and beyond so that we progressed less than a mile in two hours. The temptation to stop and build a fire was great. Jack never complained. He was bleeding from deep scratches along his arms and face and dripped with orange slime having keeled over more than once in the quagmire. But always he kept going; never a complaint.

He was not given to philosophy nor did he talk much except when the conversation was of the regiment or home life. He had a crinkled photograph of his pretty Scots wife; very petite with a mischievous elfin face. Their baby Jason was a few months old and 'wee Aggis' his wife had written him disturbing letters that he must leave the Army as she could not bear being away from him. Jack became determined to emigrate to British Columbia—where he had been promised a good job at Fireside—he planned to buy himself out of the Army once we returned home.

Before joining the Scots Greys he had been fat and lazy but skiing and running were now his favourite sports. He was from a small mining village in Midlothian and had moved from one pre-fab house to another as his father changed jobs. He had never mixed well, not even with his three brothers: they had liked to wander the streets from café to café. He had always loved the woods and solitary rambles with his dog.

I began to get dizzy spells again and the sores on my back and shoulders complained fiercely each time the metal pack frame shifted. Despite his own state, Jack said he would take the radio back. We argued for a while but finally I let him have it. We moved extremely slowly and had no energy now to force a way through the undergrowth nor pull our legs clear from the clinging swamp.

What would have happened had we taken any other route or followed a different bearing is difficult to assess but our chances of extricating ourselves from that endless nightmare were remote. The labyrinth of entwined valleys made a mockery of direction-finding for one had to follow their meanderings rather than a compass bearing in order to avoid the mountains and ravines.

Late in the evening we waded through huge dead tree trunks half-submerged in open swamp and came to a ridge of higher ground, along which ran a game trail leading north-east. This was wonderful but we had long since learned to quash all feelings of hope, since every time we had come to good ground, it had petered out after a short while. I remember thinking it strange that there should be footprints in this remote region and fairly recent ones too.

We must have trudged along for a full five minutes gazing in half-hearted interest at the bootprints before common sense began to assert itself through the fog of exhaustion.

'Hey, Ran, d'ye no think these bootprints could be ours?'

We stopped and checked and they were. The relief was considerable. It had been hell being lost in such country with no hope of escape from the bone-chilling cold. Now we could retrace our tracks to Skook's.

We followed the trail and there was no longer any doubt. We began to recognise certain markings and then saw a deep tree-blaze.

The trail which had earlier seemed so inadequate and difficult, now —after days in the undergrowth—appeared to us like a motorway.

By the end of August we were back at the Forsberg Ridge and Jack managed to contact the Mounties at Attlin—200 miles away beyond the Cassiars. He asked them to contact RCMP Watson Lake to prevent any aerial searches being mounted.

When we reached the Kechika at the Frog River cabins we put the battered portable canoe together and paddled downriver to Skook's, a distance of some thirty miles. The journey was exhilarating. There were snags and drift-piles to avoid and the rucksacks made the canoe unwieldy, we sprung a leak and bailed out on the move with our cooking pot, but the joy of moving fast and being able to sit made these seem very minor problems.

And so, after a long and weary journey, we had failed.

Both of us felt like a long rest but that could not be unless the expedition as a whole was to founder. We must get more rations sent by air from Watson Lake and set out again at once. Luckily for us Moira Farrow of the *Vancouver Sun* was already at Watson Lake with a photographer. She now said she would fly to Skook's and bring our rations.

Also at Skook's were Joe and Stan. Both looked pale and Joe's back was still paining him but he had been able to shoot a moose for the old man's larder and do some odd jobs around the place. They had had a hair-raising journey by canoe down the Kechika after we had parted in the forest, for they had been sucked into a log jam. Their canoe and most of their equipment had sunk immediately but they had escaped, built a great fire on the bank until they had thawed out and then struck off on foot north along the trail which runs beside the river from Gataga Forks to Skook's land.

Skook could not understand how we had missed the river trail and again reiterated that there were no other blazed routes, so we decided to set out again on the trail the next day. The Irish doctor taped up Jack's ankle and told him that he was stupid to walk further on it but Jack was adamant. Before departing we gorged ourselves on a gargantuan meal; we set to on sunnyside eggs, pancakes and maple syrup, blueberry pie and moose steak; all washed down with rich sweet coffee. As all our clothes were wet we borrowed some from Orville the Indian and snuggled down for the night in the warmth of the cookhouse cabin with the mice and an old snoring husky.

Next morning there were ten degrees of frost outside and our aches, blisters and open sores made the thought of the packs most unwelcome: they weighed under sixty pounds which, though heavy, was quite manageable. This time we took rations, campkit, clothes and first aid equipment. We left the radio, rifle, canoe and ropes for Joe and Stan to take out with them on the weekly seaplane.

After thanking Skook and promising to send him 'a thick English blanket' we limped off along a horse trail that led to Gataga Forks. I soon began to feel that there was something wrong with Jack. Normally he was never more than two or three yards behind but now he was lagging and limping badly. I stopped till he caught up but it happened again. We had been three miles or so and the trail was excellent.

It was his ankle. Despite the bandages it was paining him worse than before and it would only court disaster for him to go on. He was obstinate, determined to continue, and had set his heart on our success. I pointed out the folly of his going any further. In all likelihood there would be no trail for many days and we might have to wade up the river itself. Its slippery stones would be no place for a weak ankle.

Finally Jack agreed and we turned back. I looked round and saw that he was crying silently. The frustration after trying so hard must have been very disappointing.

Later, at Skook's, we parted by the creek and Jack wished me luck giving me his own blanket and pistol.

I followed the Kechika River for fifteen miles to its junction with the Gataga. The trail petered out in the bushes by the confluence. Without a canoe, I tried wading across but the river was too swift and deep. I could not risk being swept away and my gear getting soaked.

Finding four small logs, I lashed them together with string and cross sticks, laying my lifejacket on the platform provided. My clothes, boots and rucksack were all wrapped in the polythene sheet and I swam across towing the raft by a plaited string line. The water was freezing but I reached the other bank only a hundred yards downstream of my startpoint.

Thawing out by a driftwood fire, I followed our trail up to the old Frog cabins, noticing the scrape marks where Joe had dragged his pack along on poles.

I slept in the least dirty of the three cabins, first removing two half-skinned wolverine pelts, an owl's wing and a quantity of moose droppings. Little rodents ran around the cabin all night and twice woke me up by gnawing at my beard and hair. In the morning my day's ration of oatmeal biscuits was gone. Where they had been was a little pile of twigs and a large fir cone: also the cabin had an evil smell about it which had not been there when I arrived. I refused to believe myself responsible for the smell but could find no other possible source. Later, in Fort Ware, an Indian told me about Pack or 'trader' rats which are long bushy-tailed wood rodents and smell disgustingly musty. Whenever they take anything, he said, they leave a gift in exchange for, after all, exchange is no robbery. He told me a tale, that he said was quite true, of an aged prospector who, returning from a fruitless three-year search in the Yukon made camp in a deserted cabin. Next morning he found his mug had been stolen and a chunk of rock left in its place. The rock contained gold quartz and the prospector made a fortune.

The morning was bitterly cold but the sky was clear. Before leaving the cabin I sprinkled the raw places on my shoulders, back and hands with penicillin powder. The sores were infected and had become quite deep so I bound them with plasters where possible.

Once the trail bore east and away from the river, I left it and inched through the foliage. After three hours I had advanced less than a mile and began to feel desperate. How long would this impossible undergrowth go on for?

Sweating like a pig, for the sun was high and the land sweltered, I forgot my sores and tore off the lifejacket, finishing off the water in one of my two water-bottles.

There had been a forest fire not long ago and the trees now lay in mad confusion, one across the other, jumbled ten feet high like a great sprawling log pyre. The trunks were charred so that soon my clothes and hands were black. Secondary growth grew thickly amongst the deadfall, much of it stunted thornbush. I tried squirming beneath the trees but the rucksack was too bulky, a thorn jabbed the inside of my ear and a great many other places, which was frustrating.

Lying jammed beneath two trunks, I felt the blood running from inside my ear and on some childish impulse cursed the trees and the whole bloody country aloud. Perhaps I was near to panic, believing that I was deaf in that ear and to make matters worse, I could see nothing, not even the high ridge of the Forsberg Mountain. I could not really remember what compass bearing to take for the river and I gulped down water from my last bottle. It was, I found, a little better moving cautiously from trunk to trunk above the undergrowth like a hunchback monkey with poor balance. Twice the charred trunks snapped beneath my weight and I plunged down through the thorns to the blackened stumps ten feet below.

By noon I had finished my water and prayed I was heading for the river. The heat was incredible. It was difficult to believe that in a few hours it would be freezing. I discovered a pool of foetid orange water—thick with floating algae. It might have been acid for all I cared. I drank deep and filled both bottles, feeling hope again.

After a long while the trees thinned out until at last I could walk unimpeded through marshy flats and down a mossy bank to the Kechika.

It was a welcome spot untouched by fire where I could boil water for tea and as I bathed in the river, I determined never to leave the Kechika's course again no matter how it meandered. That afternoon the going was good at first with plenty of well-marked game trails so that by dusk I could make out the Forsberg Ridge but lightning was flashing in the Cassiars and a thunderstorm seemed to be coming my way. I splashed through a swamp by torchlight, cutting quickly towards the hills to find high, dry ground before the storm broke. But the marsh climbed too so I pushed desperately on, for my polythene sheet must be up before the rains came.

Jack above the Frog River where two of the men are injured.

The author's raft and baggage at Gataga Forks

We strain to escape the great log jam closing in on the craft on Williston Lake.

A slalom course through the drowning forest.

The torch batteries were dim and the marsh deceptive. The thunder sounded all around and, finding a low clump of alder on a lonely tumulus I lashed the sheeting carefully over a horizontal alder pole some four feet from the ground and in the centre of the clump.

No sooner was my little tent up than the clouds burst. The rain came in a great vertical sheet drumming against the polythene as though it would flatten it into the marsh that wallowed all around the tiny hummock. The thunder went but the rain fell heavily most of the night, wetting all the wood so I had to cook over hexamin fuel blocks.

All around as far as I could see the ground was silvery with water as though the marsh was a lake. Perhaps it was. Exhausted, I slept soundly. All my cuts were weeping poison in the morning so I cleaned them with iodine and put on fresh plasters.

After many miles of marsh there was forest. Twice I was over-joyed to find a well-blazed trail moving high above the Kechika. This must be Skook's trail: everything would be easy now, I felt — but each time it petered out in muskeg or rocky creekbeds.

It was no good simply crossing the obstacles in the hope that the trail would continue on the far side, for this was usually not the case.

For two days the forest closed me in, allowing only the occasional glimpse of the Rockies looming over the valley. Sometimes, finding the trail, I could move fifteen miles and more in a day, but without it, I would flounder through the soaking undergrowth for long hours on a compass bearing, zigzagging up steep slopes between the river and the mountains to find the trail again.

On the fifth day I estimated that the Sifton Pass could not be more than ten miles ahead. I followed the trail to the river where it faded out. It was raining as usual and I stopped for, although there were still three hours of daylight I was feeling dizzy, lightheaded and very tired.

I ate more penicillin tablets and fell asleep on the bank where a small clearing contained the rotten logs of a long derelict cabin. I awoke after a while shivering violently and feeling very sick.

K   145

Digging beneath a fallen tree trunk, I found some dry moss and twigs which ignited with the help of peeled birch bark.

A helicopter moved low over the forest following the river. I fired two red miniflares and it landed in the clearing.

The pilot introduced himself as Bill Johnson. He was surprised to see me saying he had never seen any sign of life in this region before. He was ferrying helicopters down from the Yukon. I offered him some tea and asked how far it was to Fox Lake.

'About twenty-eight to thirty miles, I guess, but I'm not too sure. I've not been this way too often. But I do know there's plenty of swamp between here and there. You'll find it real hard going if it's only half as bad as it looks from the air, friend.'

It was getting dark so the man took his leave.

I had put my polythene sheet up by the side of the clearing: the draught from the heliblades tore it down and blew it into the trees.

Only another thirty miles at most. This was good news but next morning there was a new problem. The trail disappeared completely and the country rose steeply from the river to the cliffs of the Rockies. Without a trail it was no longer possible to move through the woods which were deeply fissured by craggy ravines. Perhaps the Indian trail-makers had been forced high into the mountains by the narrow declivity of the river valley at this point. Feeling this could be the only answer — since Skook had often repeated that the trail never crossed to the west of the river — I toiled up to 5,000 feet; above the treeline.

Once a brown bear crashed through the undergrowth not thirty yards away and I stood motionless, breathing heavily. It must have been frightened off by my tin cooking pots which clanked together as I moved. I had hoped that their noise would prevent a chance meeting with a bear or moose. And anyway the homely clanging provided a friendly sound in the deep silence of the forests.

When the trees gave way to straggly bush and finally bald rock walls I gave up. The Indians could hardly have made a trail any higher: they were down-to-earth Sikanees after all, not cliff-hanging Aztecs.

That night I was back again in the clearing eating another day's precious rations but with nothing to show for it.

At dawn, with my rucksack wrapped in the polythene sheet, I waded up the Kechika holding onto branches where possible. On either side the cliffs rose steeply for 400 feet to the forest.

The soil was loose alluvial gravel much given to rockfalls: mountain streams had in many places cut through the glacial residue and down into the rock, shaping new ravines. The upper ramparts of these cemented gravel canyons formed curiously eroded, almost animated, figures known as hoodoos. I felt, through their eerie presence, as if under permanent observation.

Towards noon the canyons changed their character, narrowing into a series of deep ravines, no longer floored by glacial drift but by a well-worn conglomerate rock of at least the Upper Cretaceous era. At once the river was deeper and faster, pouring over a succession of long ledges. I was swept over, and, wet through, attempted to half-flounder, half-swim. This was impossible with the cumbersome pack, and the river might continue through such canyons for ten miles or more.

Deciding to cut my losses before catching pneumonia I waded back to the clearing dejectedly.

The poisonous area of my back and shoulders had begun to throb due to immersion in the icy Kechika. I heated water, poured it into the cloth-covered water-bottle and pressed it against the sore places.

Without enough rations to return to Skook's, unable to move up the river or along the bank, I felt suddenly very old, ill, and inept. Also a little frightened: I had no wish to starve and shiver to a slow death in this godforsaken forest.

In the afternoon a small aeroplane flew up the Trench. It looked like the Cessna from Watson Lake Air Services—probably calling for something at Fort Ware. It would be back in an hour or so.

I knew then that I must attract its attention on its return flight. Let them know that something was wrong. After all there would be no more lucky breaks with river-hopping helicopters.

Sure enough the plane came back after an hour, about 2,000 feet up and slightly west of overhead. By then I had a good fire going with wet logs providing plenty of smoke. My orange anorak and silver Arctic blanket were laid out in the clearing, and I fired two mini flares. There was no sun, so mirror-flashing was out of the question.

The plane flew on and soon disappeared. It might be a week before another one came.

I looked over at the far bank. Dense clumps of alder, willow and soupalalie crowded the river. Then the foothills of the Cassiars rising high and clad in tangled vegetation of spruce, balsam, poplar and jackpine. Somehow the land seemed to roll more gently over there.

The grass of course is always greener on the other side of the wall but I thought I would give it a try. Should I wade across and try the other side of the valley there would be no trail; everyone — and the map too — agreed over that, but perhaps the going would be easier with many game trails. With luck I might then make five miles a day to the south and be at Fox Lake in six days. I had food enough for two days which would have to be rationed carefully.

At first the undergrowth was appalling but, a thousand feet or so above the river, there was a forested ridge running south-west. I spent the night on the ridge: it was colder than ever and my back hurt intolerably.

Around dawn I could bear the cold no longer and built a fire beside my shelter. I fell asleep then in its glorious warmth and did not wake until long after sun-up, startled by the raucous croaking of a Whisky Jack, a small grey jay-bird often known as the Camp-Robber through its audacious attacks on Canadian tourists' picnics.

I felt extremely hungry but the jay stayed out of range and since it was only half the size of a fool-hen, I was not tempted to waste ·38 bullets trying to bag it.

My back felt tender but the throbbing had gone. Towards noon I found a well-used game trail with fresh moose and wolf spoor in evidence. Once I came upon the still-steaming urine of some large animal. I shouted into the undergrowth ahead and after a hundred yards or so, found a long skid mark — probably a moose that had been startled by my yells. My permanent fear was that of rounding a bend in the narrow trail and meeting a bear. The grizzlies stand over eight feet tall and have four-inch claws. If cornered or frightened they will attack at once and a pistol would not be much better than a pea-shooter by way of despatching an irate grizzly.

Like the smaller black bears, grizzlies eat anything from berries and roots to fish and moosemeat. They raid anthills for ants, nests for eggs, and beehives for honey, their fur being too thick for bee stings—or ·38 bullets—to do much damage. Throughout western Canada many bears are shot each year for breaking into houses and stores to loot all available food. Not just what they can smell either, for they've learnt that odourless boxes and tins often contain the humans' most delicious goodies.

Being basically idle, bears become beggars very easily. If when chancing upon a cabin or a road they are thrown edible scraps they will come back daily for more, forsaking their normal laborious ways of finding food. Because there are some ten million summer tourists along British Columbia's relatively few roads, many bears learn to trade their photogenic qualities for summer scraps, but they quickly become disgruntled when winter halts the flow of tourists and the country returns to its indigenous population of less than three million. Thereafter they approach pedestrians who, unlike motorists, are not so keen on handing out food to over-friendly bears. This infuriates the bruins who will often decide to punish the thoughtless hiker with one gentle but nonetheless neckbreaking blow of their forepaw.

The game trail met others and I noticed strange blaze marks on certain trees. Some appeared to have been scratched by bearclaws but others might well have been scraped by Indians. Then I saw a clearly marked triple cut—one slash above the other—which in Sikanee territory indicates a nearby trapping line. Very soon the trail merged with others at a narrow strip of marsh. On the other side I saw with great pleasure a single horizontal log. Its end had been cleanly sawn off: I was back on an—or the—Indian trail down the Trench.

Forgetting hunger, sores and blisters, I set off at a fast pace. I was at a loss to explain my good luck in the light of Skook's advice and the evidence of my map. Perhaps, since the handful of Indians who use the trail do not need maps, and since no white men had used the route for at least twenty years, the old trail to the east of the river had been destroyed by landslides in the hoodoo region and the Indians had been forced to cross the river to continue the trail on the west side of the valley.

The path snaked through flat marshland amongst dense clumps of willow and alder and sparse glades of tamarack. Many wild flowering plants grew in scattered clearings thick with berry bushes—cranberry, raspberry, gooseberry, and blueberry—and a carpet of tiny strawberry plants covered any hummock where the drainage was good. The place teemed with wildlife and I adjusted my tins to swing quietly. There were many pools and streams which hardly moved at all. Somewhere round here the headwaters of the Kechika would rise, beyond which all water would flow south: only then would I know I had reached the Pass.

This was good trapping country, abundant with beaver, marten, fisher, otter, and mink. Many of the pools were hundreds of yards wide and I had no option but to wade through them cursing the beavers whose dams were to blame. Besides the scattered beaver lodges there were the smaller more compact mud domes of the semi-nomadic muskrats or musquash, 'mink-fodder' as the Indians call them. They had no visible entrance holes so presumably the furry rats get in and out via submerged tunnels. The thought of a roasted muskrat brought back the pangs of hunger for they are reputed to be delicious. I lost the trail in the marsh but this was no longer important for the scrub gave way to a wide open swamp meadow enclosed by rising forest.

Beyond the meadow all water moved south. I had reached Latitude fifty-eight degrees where the Sifton Pass, at 3,273 feet, forms the headwaters of the Fox or Tochieka River, Ka being Indian for River, Tochie meaning the Fox.

For some strange reason which I failed to understand the Indians had laid their trail in the centre of the valley and close to the Fox, so that it crossed through the middle of several bogs, but this mattered little for—once over the Pass—the trail was well worn and quite wide. Obviously the family of Indians at Fox Lake were accustomed to hunt and trap around the swamps of the Pass.

Now I could average three miles an hour and late in the afternoon I rounded a bend in the trail to see Jack and Joe Skibinski out hunting squirrels.

Both seemed rather quiet. Four miles further south, the trail nudged the shore of a wide lake at the far end of which were the little cabins of the McCook family of Indians.

A mile along the bank from the cabins on a narrow beach of shingle were the blue BBC tents and a communal tent they had made from a tarpaulin lent by the Indians. They too were somewhat subdued and I sensed something was very wrong. But for a while I thought, problems of morale will have to wait: Ginnie had sent rations and fresh food for all by seaplane. A separate packet was earmarked for Jack and me. For a full half-hour I gorged myself until I could eat no more and then suffered the expert ministrations of Stanley, the medic, to my back and shoulders.

It was only forty miles or so to Fort Ware and the trail, said the McCooks, was good. Joe and Stanley were not fit enough yet but Jack, though still limping like a constipated crab, was determined to complete the journey to Fort Ware.

I spoke to him alone soon afterwards. He was feeling very bitter about the others who had been anything but friendly since his own arrival by seaplane from Skook's. Joe and Stanley, disappointed within themselves at having to turn back, had arrived at Fox Lake to find the BBC in a very acid mood. After a week or so they had found themselves under the thrall of the BBC and, as Joe pointed out to me some weeks after our return to Britain, it was difficult for him not to feel their influence for they were after all something very special, almost romantic; winners of international documentary film awards – the men who made entertainment for millions.

Why Richard and Paul were so disgruntled I was soon to find out.

Meanwhile Jack declared himself perfectly ready to leave as soon as I had rested. We inspected the map and asked the Indians if the trail was clearly marked.

All the male Indians were away guiding big-game hunters but one tough-looking young woman—who had recently tried to knife a visiting Indian named Nick Prince—said she would be prepared to guide us to Fort Ware since she wanted to go there anyway. After much wrangling we settled upon the sum of twenty-five dollars a day as her fee and she agreed to be ready the following morning. We pointed out that her fee was extortionate, she maintained that it was ridiculously cheap and that we could go and get lost if we wanted. Since this observation was very near to the bone we demurred and determined that come what may we would make Fort Ware in a day's travel.

Back at camp I spread my polythene sheet between some spruce and cooked an enormous stew. Richard detached himself from the camp fire where Ben and Joe were muttering in between gulps of beer. He came over to my bush and for a full ten minutes gave vent to his feelings. All his old worries about early reveilles and late camps on the Nahanni were regurgitated as were a hundred and one administrative complaints. But his main bugbear—which was behind the latent antagonism I had sensed since arriving—was the mistaken opinion that news had somehow reached the Canadian and British press that Jack and I were lost in the heart of the Rockies.

Richard and Paul, being highly conscientious at their work, were gripped by the nightmare vision of returning to London to face their BBC boss Chris Brasher and having to admit that they had absolutely no film to cover what—isolated at Fox Lake—they had presumed to be headlines all over Britain. Had this been the case, their anguish and bitterness might have been justified, but in fact only the Canadian papers had reported our mountain wanderings—which would in any case have been most unphotogenic in the gloomy forests of the Kechika Valley and the endless rain of the Rockies.

However, at the time, I too, was ignorant of what news had reached Britain, and so could only murmur sweet nothings of appeasement to mollify Richard's feelings. After all it was very natural for him to be worried about the film; he had much at stake. Also it could not have been inspiring waiting here week after week in the pouring rain with a dehydrated diet varied only by the

occasional rabbit and trout. The compensation of beautiful Fox
Lake and its surroundings had long since worn off.

The Fox River itself was no more than a fast-running stream
blocked in many places by deadfall and decaying roots. That it
flowed through a beautiful region of high truncated spurs and
hanging valleys, pot-hole lakes and morainal piles from long-
departed glaciers, impressed no one just then.

Our Indian guide packed her few belongings in a double-sided
cloth panier which she lashed on the back of a powerful-looking
husky dog. She wore light slip-on shoes, jeans and an old denim
jacket and carried a battered ·22 rifle under her arm.

Pocahontas and her hound Tomahawk led the way through a
spider's web of forest trails; only her name was Eileen McCook and
her dog was called Rover. As Jack and I walked she talked over her
shoulder of the grizzly bears her brothers were hunting in the
mountains, of the timber wolves that roamed these valleys in packs
of thirty when winter food was scarce. The trail was excellent and
the forest as free from windfall and undergrowth as an English
wood. Jack's ankle was well strapped up and Stanley had massaged
it liberally with embrocation.

High above us, as we plodded along, a Beaver droned north: the
plane that would take the others to Fort Ware.

Eileen had walked these trails since she was tiny; indeed it was the
McCook family and no one else who kept them open.

John, leader of the McCooks, had spent many days felling tall
pines over the Fox and its tributaries so that, though we crossed the
winding river many times it was seldom necessary to wade. Some
of the 'bridges' were very narrow and slippery so Rover the husky
needed much encouragement by way of a gentle boot on his backside
before he would mount and cross them.

He seemed to suffer from vertigo and would obviously have
preferred to have swum. This we were most anxious to prevent
since we would have been duty bound to offer Eileen one of our
sleeping-bags had hers been soaked by an amphibious Rover.
He was wont to travel just behind Eileen. From time to time, usually
when least expected, he would scent some bird or animal and stop

dead. Jack would trip over him and I over Jack. Eileen found this most amusing. Once we came upon a putrefying squirrel lying on the trail. Rover scooped it up without actually pausing in his stride and gulped it down whole. For an hour or so afterwards he gave vent to an alarming series of staccato belches that sounded almost human.

In a clearing we came to a village of the dead where a number of long kennel-like buildings—outsize doll's houses—had been built over the graves of dead Indians; Eileen's ancestors.

Eileen never seemed to tire but we were pleased to shrug off our rucksacks shortly before midnight after ascending and descending a high mesa-topped ridge that stretched across the valley. I found it too cold to sleep and kept the fire going all night. Long before dawn I made porridge from biscuits and salt and woke the others. We had walked twenty-one miles the day before so there were fifteen to go before 9.30 a.m. if we were to complete the journey in twenty-four hours—which was most necessary since I could only afford twenty-five dollars.

Jack spilled the porridge in the dark so we scooped the grey gunge back into the pot spiced with pine needles and clogged up with ants. This we ate with great relish but Eileen found it unpalatable.

'Wrggh,' muttered Jack into his porridge, 'a horrible thing happened last night. I woke to find a wee moose running all o'er me heed. I wapped it one wi me fist and it went, but I can still remember the feel o' it.' He shuddered expressively.

Eileen stared at him in horror.

'I think you try to pull my leg, Jackie. Or mebbe you have a bad dream for there are no moose-wah tracks in this place.'

After four hours we came to a blackened region of wide devastation. 'Many miles of land are burned all the way to the far mountains,' Eileen explained. 'It happen in the big fires in 1964 when all our traplines are destroyed and the forests too as far as one mile from Fort Ware. One more mile and everything would have gone. Already the outside walls of our homes were too hot to touch. We poured water over them all the time for a spark would be enough to start them burning.'

In twenty-four hours almost to the minute we reached the village and thanked Eileen, wondering how much of the twenty-five dollars would be spent on drinking hooch and how much for food for her family back at Fox Lake.

The Tochieka-Fox pours into the Finlay River with a powerful rush and close by the confluence was Fort Ware, a line of low cabins close to the waterfront.

The long trek was over. Now only 900 miles of water and the fearsome Fraser Rapids separated us from our goal.

9

Over the Great Divide

A YOUNG INDIAN NAMED PADDY POOLE HAD HIS WRIST SLIT WIDE open, tendons and all. That was the day we came to Fort Ware.

Bill Van Somers the storesman, trader, and general councillor of all the Ware Indians at once radioed Mackenzie for an emergency seaplane. Fortunately the message was received—for his radio telephone was largely dependent on mist-and storm-free atmospherics—and Bill had flown off to hospital with the injured man.

Before leaving, he had arranged for all our equipment to be stored in his boathouse on the bank of the Finlay. The others had already flown in from Fox Lake and begun to prepare the boats and stores all of which Ginnie had sent up by riverboat some days earlier from faraway Mackenzie. After their long sojourn at Fox Lake, the BBC were pleased to be on the move again and their morale seemed better.

A tiny Cessna Supercub seaplane splashed down on the Finlay. The senior Roman Catholic padre of British Columbia was touring the northern parishes with Father McCormick, the local flying priest. His flock was scattered far and wide in settlements and reserves from Babine to Fox Lake; a farflung network of little parishes that he could only visit regularly by flying hundreds of miles over forest and mountain to land on the nearest lake or river. Beside Fort Ware's compact log church was a schoolhouse where many of the younger Indian children studied under the supervision of a married white couple; both teachers from the Department of

Indian Affairs. The elder children were flown off to a boarding school in Prince George.

On a high rise above the church, with a panoramic view of the Finlay River and the far southern ranges, the Indian dead slept in rows of wooden kennels. They are not really dead, their kinsfolk believe, and their spirits are kept happy after burial by the insertion of favourite possessions into their kennels: a clay pipe perhaps, some beads or maybe a rusty rifle. The birds, the wolves and the elements are also kept at bay by the little shelters. One was slightly apart from the others, that of Chief Davie, after whom Skook had named the so-called trail.

Chief Davie had originally been the leader of the Finlay River Indians and when the river began to rise in the 1960s because of the new man-made dam on Williston Lake, he had brought his Indians up to the nearest Hudson's Bay Company Store which was at Fort Ware. Chief Davie's immediate descendants proved, to my surprise, to be the McCooks. It is quite likely that the McCooks do have some Scottish blood in their veins because many of the early pioneers in the region were Scotsmen who often took squaws into their keeping to while away the long winters and to look after daily chores. But the Scottish surname does not necessarily point to a 'white' taint in their lineage, since a few generations ago, most Indians Europeanised their names for the sake of convenience. Some took the name of the local priest or trader and others translated or altered their former Indian names into anglicised versions. Most have still kept an Indian name as well, but it is only used on rare ceremonial occasions.

This constant need to adapt to white civilisation has sapped most of the Indians of their vitality; puritanical missionaries have taken much of the colour and enthusiasm out of their lives and most of their old way of life has been destroyed. Already ravaged by several decades of disease, alcohol and gunpowder, overpowered by massive theologies, the Indians had been no great force to reckon with when the first settlers began to arrive. At Fort Ware we saw few relics of the old cultures and much evidence of the contemporary malaise.

Father McCormick and the schoolteachers tried hard, but there was too little for the Indians to do; nothing to ward off apathy. They flocked to see the Father's monthly film show and there was great interest in his proposed river ice rink for the winter months for which he had already brought in a quantity of ice skates. Father McCormick felt strongly that the Indians were searching for an identity and needed something rewarding to occupy them in order for them to regain their pride. They had lost their self-respect along with their age-old winter ceremonies and potlatch feasts, their complex dances, totems and oratory. No longer did they need beautifully made masks and the fabulous totem poles which formed their family crests. Now the young folk despised the traditional trappings as outmoded. Winklepicker shoes and cowboy hats were in, traplines and potlatch out. Even the Chiefs were elected by vote so that the hereditary chieftains were mere non-functional figureheads.

I walked along the riverbank to the teachers' house with Dave Ransom, a sub-contracting carpenter who was building cabins for the Indian Affairs Department. He told me never, but *never*, to walk alone in the dark in Fort Ware. He then proceeded to tell me gruesome and alarming tales about the local Indians whom he employed. One quiet smiling log-caulker had murdered his own father and another had been knifed by his girl-friend clean through the stomach and lungs. The trouble was drink which they would concoct from anything they could lay their hands on, yeast, dates, sugar, carrots, maple syrup, even hair oil. It often made them blind and their limbs swelled up, then they became wild and beat up anyone who was around.

When we reached the teachers' house, Lou the wife, welcomed us with coffee. The two priests were also there and we sat round in the shack talking about the Indians. Evidently two years ago a rumour had spread in the outside world that the Indians at Fort Ware were cut off from their monthly supply boat by storms and huge log jams; that they were dying from lack of food. It was quite untrue but once the word was out a ton or more of food supplies arrived by plane. This just lay on the riverbank for a long while; some of it rotted, the rest got turned into hooch.

Whilst we were gossiping, Father McCormick was called out by a young girl called Fanny McCook. Later the Father returned looking flustered: he had had to intervene between a tough young drunken Indian and Fanny's eleven-year-old little sister whom the Indian was bent on raping. I asked the Father if he were not afraid of the man assaulting him. He said indeed he was but he'd tried to keep out of range. But, he said, remember that it was the whites who introduced the alcohol which is now just about the only solace available to the Indians and it was the white man who took away their dignity. Listening to the priests and the schoolteachers chatting away in that cabin I realised how much each of them had given up to help these charming but wayward Indians of the north.

One of the stories they told concerned Monica Storrs, a most zealous envangelist who had arrived in Fort Ware in the late 1930s, She was the forty-year-old maiden daughter of a Cathedral Close family at Winchester who had inherited £40,000 on her father's death with which she had emigrated to the Peace River, saying that she had been 'called' there in a vision. She had walked to the Peace River along the Edson Trail from Dawson and on arrival had built herself a cabin which she named The Abbey. She had never ridden a horse before but now she proceeded to travel all over Peace River country on an old nag spreading the Gospel, acting as midwife and founding Bible Camps in places like Charlie Lake which she called the Sea of Galilee. On one of her summer journeys to Fort Ware, her outboard motor gave out and knowing nothing about engines, she spent many days wading through shallows, punting the boat or clinging to the stern, threshing her feet about in the water, until one day she kicked the motor in disgust—after which it started with ease. Ever since that day, the story goes, Canadians have called outboard motors 'kickers'. When Miss Storrs' workload finally got too great she sent for more unmarried daughters of the English clergy. Four duly arrived who travelled far and wide through the land and soon became known as Miss Storrs' Galloping Virgins.

Later that night, back in the boathouse where the snow-laden wind squeezed through the uncaulked planking, I dossed down on the concrete floor. Long after midnight I was woken by two powerfully built Indians; both very drunk. One, a darkly handsome fellow with a flat Asian face, introduced himself as 'Alec'. His friend, by torchlight, was unusually ugly and tottered from side to side as though he would collapse over my sleeping-bag.

Flurries of fine snow gusted through the door which they had left open and my teeth began to chatter. However, I spoke pleasantly to the two men for it occurred to me that the larger one went by the same name as the would-be rapist whom Father McCormick had earlier confronted and who was said to be handy with a knife.

After a very cold hour's slurred conversation to which my only contribution was the intermittent and fervent muttering of Yes — Yes; both Indians shook my hand and with a great many hooch-laden salutations lurched out of the boathouse leaving the door open.

Next day a Beaver of Northern Thunderbird Airlines flew in and moored to a riverboat. As usual the Indians came running in their colourful shirts and tight jeans to line the bank above the floatplane.

Bryn Campbell jumped out, cameras flying and a broad grin creasing his face with its bushy rim of jet-black beard. He had completed his assignment in Europe and was eager to be back on the water — providing the log jams were few and far between.

Ginnie had come too, for it was our first wedding anniversary and the plane was to spend an hour in Ware before returning to Mackenzie.

Her news was none too good. The Fraser was indeed far worse than the Nahanni: everyone had told her grim stories of giant whirlpools and fatal capsizes. And there would be problems with Williston Lake. We must watch out for sudden storms, submerged ice-sharpened stakes, and an enormous log jam at the northern end of the Lake which, from the air, had appeared to stretch unbroken across its entire width. The Lake continues south for 200 miles, its northern end being the flooded Finlay River, the southern part the Parsnip which, flowing north, meets the Finlay at Finlay Forks where both rivers join as the Peace to cut east through the Rockies.

Once at the southernmost end of the Lake, where the Parsnip enters it, we would have to find the mouth of the tiny Pack River and, moving against the current, follow it and its tributary, the Crooked

River, to Summit Lake. Furthermore, owing to our troubles along the Kechika, we would arrive behind schedule at the Pack and Crooked Rivers. So there would in all probability be too little water for our inflatables to manœuvre against the current. Already we had used far more than the estimated amount of fuel provided by BP. Much of this had been swallowed up by the greedy Canadian army lorry which averaged five miles to the gallon. As a result the driver, Corporal Wally Wallace, had driven it back over the Rockies to Alberta and returned it to its unit. He had then flown to Germany for a promotion course and his place was taken by an old friend of Ginnie's named Sarah Salt.

She had been summoned by telegram from a holiday in Italy and was now driving a Land-Rover lent us by British Leyland, Vancouver.

After a brief hour together, Ginnie left in the Beaver to join Sarah Salt at Mackenzie. There they would await our arrival by boat.

We would set off down the clear blue Finlay River in the morning. The Finlay River rises in Thutade Lake and roars south through canyons, over cataracts and waterfalls until it reaches Ware. Then it flows for 150 miles into the newly made Williston Lake. All the waters in this Lake now flow over the W. A. C. Bennett Dam into the Peace River. But in the old days, before this dam and man-made lake were formed, the Finlay flowed south until it met up with the Parsnip River coming in from the south at Finlay Forks, whereupon these two rivers merged and flowed due east into the Peace River which in turn emptied, and still empties, into the great Mackenzie and thence to the Arctic. It is 2,525 miles long from the Finlay to the Arctic, the longest waterway in North America after the Mississippi and the Missouri.

In 1793 Alexander Mackenzie, an explorer for the North West Company followed a route from the Arctic to Finlay Forks. He was the first white man to see the Finlay, after which he turned south up the Parsnip and eventually reached the Pacific by a roundabout route and become the first man to cross the continent to the western ocean.

The year before, another Scot of the same company had built a

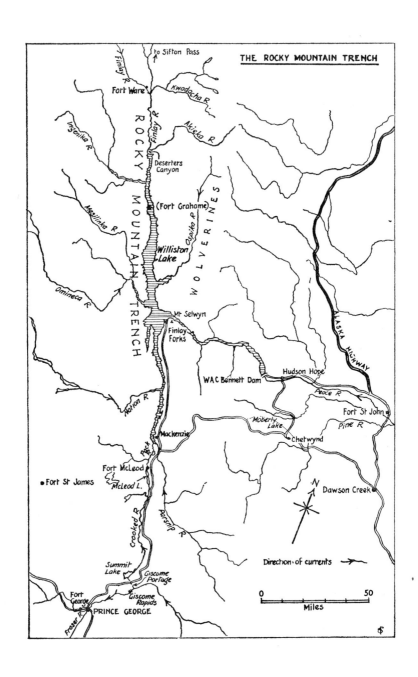

THE ROCKY MOUNTAIN TRENCH

to Sifton Pass

Finlay R.

Fort Ware

Kwadacha R.

R
O
C
K
Y

Akieka R.

Ingenika R.

R
o
s
e
r
R

Deserters
Canyon

(Fort Grahame)

Mesilinka R.

M
O
U
N
T
A
I
N

Osilinka R.

Williston
Lake

W
O
L
V
E
R
I
N
E
S

Omineca R.

T
R
E
N
C
H

Mt Selwyn

Finlay
Forks

ALASKA HIGHWAY

Nation R.

WAC Bennett Dam

Hudson Hope

Peace R.

Fort St John

Moberly
Lake

Pine R.

Mackenzie

Chetwynd

Fort St James

Fort McLeod

Pack R.

McLeod L.

Parsnip R.

N

Dawson Creek

Crooked R.

Summit
Lake

Giscome
Portage

Giscome
Rapids

Fort
George

PRINCE GEORGE

Fraser R.

Direction of currents ➤

0   50
Miles

fort on the Peace River for Mackenzie. This was John Finlay after whom the river is wrongly named.

In 1797 he went up the Finlay for seventy-five miles—less than a third of its length—but it was a much later and more celebrated expedition which succeeded in reaching Thutade Lake; the 1824 expedition which, history relates, was led by John Finlay of the North West Company.

But the history books are wrong, probably because of the corruption of Hudson's Bay Company records due to official prejudice against the real Finlay explorer, another Scot named Samuel Black, who led the 1824 expedition.

Black was a hard man and efficient but he was no trained surveyor. Despite the overall success of his 1824 journey in tracing the Finlay to its source, he made no maps. Indeed he did not even carry a compass so the tangible results of his expedition were small. This later made it easy for Black's enemies to scour his name from the Hudson's Bay Company official records of the expedition and replace it with the little known name of John Finlay.

Quite why anyone should wish to tamper with the Hudson's Bay Company records in this way is understandable only in the light of the deep-rooted rivalry and hatred which existed for so long between the competing trade companies of the north: a struggle which involved murder, arson, and corruption. The relatively small XY Company was soon exterminated but the Nor'Westers and the Hudson's Bay Company men continued their fight over furs and territory until 1821 when the former finally capitulated and were taken over by the Hudson's Bay Company.

Black's own history reveals the extent of hostility between the two companies. He became a clerk at the North West Company's Athabaska base in 1806 and then moved to Isle à la Crosse where he instigated a flare-up with the opposition. The staff of both posts tried to massacre one another and each retired with their corpses. Later, Black managed to capture the Hudson's Bay Company post and imprisoned the staff. Encouraged by his success he organised a raid on the Hudson's Bay Company fort at Green Lake ninety miles away where he overpowered the inmates and plundered all the furs.

In 1818, Black was promoted to factor at Fort Chippewan where he arrested the Lake Athabaska boss of the Hudson's Bay Company and imprisoned him for eight months before ordering him to leave the region.

A police constable was later sent to arrest the highhanded Black but retired at pistol point. When the Hudson's Bay Company finally won the day, they would doubtless have liked to sack many such old enemies as Black but could not afford to lose efficient men with a sound knowledge of the north-west. Thus he was elevated to Hudson Bay chief at Fort St John until it was abandoned in 1823 following the Indian massacre of five of the whites there.

So in 1824 Black was free for the great endeavour which would have made his name and implanted it on the map but for the long and bitter memories of the Hudson's Bay Company officials whose records became history.

After Black, no one visited the Finlay for nearly forty years when the lure of gold brought a giant Cornish miner to its banks and in 1914 Swannell the surveyor mapped the Finlay to its headwaters.

* * *

Dodging sharp ridges of rock and high drift-piles soon after leaving Fort Ware, we passed by a narrow tributary called the Kwadacha which means White Water in Indian. It ran fast with the cloudy texture of milk and for many miles refused to blend with the clear blue Finlay so that one could move downstream with totally different coloured waters flowing past either side of the boat.

The Kwadacha comes from the icefields of the Lloyd George range, its waters cleaving the Warneford or Wolverine Mountains and all the while churning a million milky particles of alluvial matter. In 1916, when outboard motors first muttered up the Finlay, an American history professor named Paul Haworth was the unlikely pioneer of the Kwadacha who first climbed above it and, looking east, spotted the vast mountain glacier that lies beyond.

All around us now the country lay wide and fertile. There seemed to be thousands of acres of good arable land, totally wild, probably once cleared by the Indians with fire: they often burnt in order to induce grass to grow but sometimes they fired whole areas through sheer devilment without a thought to the game.

The Finlay was dropping slowly so we passed much floating driftwood. Conversely, when a river is rising, it is slightly higher in the centre and drops away towards the banks: only infinitesimally but enough to cause all flotsam to catch against the banks and form drift-piles. Thus the spring floods with their vicious torrents tear away whole sections of the gravel bank, trees and all, and each year the Finlay plays havoc within its valley, resting only in the summer when the Arctic trout swim upstream.

Gradually the river valley narrowed and the water moved faster until, quite suddenly, we came to Deserters Canyon where a huge belt of black conglomerate rock crossed the Finlay Valley at right angles and squeezed the river through a narrow ravine beset with great boulders. Once, before the damming of Williston Lake caused the water to rise within the canyon, the rapids here were too fierce for even the largest canoe or riverboat. When explorer Black reached the forbidding walls of the canyon, one of his guides was drowned and two of his canoe voyagers deserted with much of the equipment, thereby giving the canyon its name. An old Indian portage trail still runs for half a mile beside the river, along the western cliff and 300 feet above the water.

A freshly painted tug, all black, grey and white, with *Forest Engineer* painted across her bows, was moored to the bank close by the northern edge of the canyon.

Jim Van Somers, the skipper, was the uncle of Bill — owner of the Fort Ware store. Following a request by Ginnie, the Forestry Service had kindly sent Jim to our aid knowing that we might have trouble with the log jams of the Lake.

Only after a long spell of northerly winds did the lake jam up so effectively but when, as now, it did so, a jostling carpet of logs blocked the whole wide expanse of water for three solid miles or more. Not a healthy environment for rubber boats.

The mess had basically been caused by inadequate clearance of the valley before it was flooded. As in many environmental catastrophes, it is difficult to apportion blame or even to say that blame should be apportioned.

Critics of the appalling condition of the lake say that more money should have been allocated both to clear the lake and to log the banks to prevent the enormous mud slides which result in tidal waves. They are sceptical of claims that the bulk of the logs will eventually become waterlogged and sink, pointing out that logs are still a menace on lakes formed twenty years ago for the Kemano-Kitimat power scheme in former Tweedsmuir Park.

Defenders of the present policy agree that money is a problem but say that the lake will be cleared in time. Karl Rieche of the Forestry Service told me that he estimated that more than three hundred million dollars would have been needed for a total log clearance and they had had to do what they could with the money available; however his Service had foreseen and planned for the reduction of flotsam and the build-up of insect populations.

A great debate is still going on about the effect that the dam is having on the ecology of the area, particularly on the moose and the fishing. But for the average Canadian the dam needs no more justification than its own success as a power plant. Although running at only half its capacity it already produced more than a million kilowatts, a third of British Columbia's hydro-electric capacity and much of it is exported to neighbouring provinces.

Population-wise there have not been any great resettlement problems in spite of the fact that the lake is British Columbia's largest, covering 640 square miles of fertile land, for there were only a handful of whites and a few dozen Indians within the reservoir area. These people have been compensated and moved to locations like Finlay Bay and Fort Ware where their life continues much as before.

The great wall which holds Williston Lake is the world's largest earth-filled dam, being half a mile thick at its base, 600 feet high and stretching for a mile and a half across the scenic Peace River Valley. The earth moving operation which all this involved was only economically feasible because of an ice formation which, several thousand years ago, forced the Peace River from its old course and into a new canyon. The same glacier later retreated and left a deep soil morained across the original riverbed and only four miles from the present dam site. When, in 1961, the excavations began, the fossils, tusks and footprints of huge dinosaurs and mammoths were found; creatures that roamed the region a hundred million years ago when it was part of a tropical swamp.

The lake was named after British Columbia's Minister of Lands, Forests and Water Resources, the Honourable Ray Williston and the dam after Social Credit Premier W. A. C. Bennett, the pleasantly puritanical hard-headed Prime Minister who ruled British Columbia for twenty years until 1972.

Later, in Vancouver, at a dinner party given for Mr Kosygin I heard one of British Columbia's Ministers telling another, 'Good old Wacky's done this province one hell of a lot of good.' The reply was down to earth. 'Wacky's OK, but God gave us the resources.' Timber alone makes British Columbia fourteen hundred million dollars a year.

*   *   *

Early in the morning we eased through the narrow rock corridors of Deserters Canyon. It was a wild and beautiful place with autumn-tinted birch and alder fringing the ochre cliffs.

Not far below the canyon where the conglomerate ridge ended abruptly, huddled the ruins of Joe Berghammer's cabin. Hamburger Joe, the other trappers used to call him in the early days. I met him later at his hut by McLeod Lake, a frazzled, toothless old man with a heavy German accent. He told me the story of one hard winter along his trapline when his toes got frostbite. All the toes of one foot. Gangrene set in and began to spread so old Joe hacked the toes off one by one with his penknife. It had been kinda sore he admitted in his quiet way but he'd lived out the winter and made it back home when spring came and the ice broke up.

Round the bend from the Berghammer place, a serried line of logs stretched right across the river which at that point became wider and was no longer confined by its banks since it had overflowed into the forest on both sides. This was the beginning of Williston Lake. The water had almost reached its intended terminal level of 2,200 feet above sea level. Once it did so, all ground beneath that height would be submerged but much of it not completely so, in that hundreds of acres of forest would remain still standing upright and only partially underwater. If a storm were to get up in such conditions, or there were an accident of some sort, we might be unable to land at all, being cut off from the true bank by dense and flooded woodland.

The three boats circled close to and upstream of the impasse. Then Jim Van Somers steamed up to the logs, the square bows of the *Forest Engineer* pushing a heavy rectangular pontoon with an iron-shod leading edge.

Slowly the little tug manœuvred until bows-on to the great jam.

Jim hooted the ship's horn as she gathered speed. Metal groaned, wood splintered and a rising back-swell rocked our boats as we watched. The tug's screw bit deep into the writhing water and the whole mass of logs shuddered ahead of her but none moved. The sturdy Perkins motors strained within the tug's belly so that she shivered from stem to stern; shaking and snarling like some blunt-nosed terrier.

Then a great shattered log rose bodily from the water behind her, mashed and spewed out by the screws. More followed and at last an undulating motion ran along the phalanx of logs. They were giving way and the *Forest Engineer* began to move in amongst them slowly but with gathering momentum as the outward concertina-movement of the logs parted a way ahead of her bows. And gingerly, like long-tailed cats in a room full of rocking chairs, we followed behind the tug.

I caught my breath as a jagged-ended log snaked past us. Stan had the engine ticking over gently and we threaded our way apprehensively forward for a hundred hazardous yards.

All the while the tug advanced, a continuous stream of scarred and broken logs shot out from behind her leaving a partially cleared and winding channel in her wake just wide enough for us to move along and dodge the murderous projectiles, any one of which, if not avoided, could have crunched right through our flimsy boats.

For an age it seemed we edged deeper into the jam, our eyes fixed on the narrow passage of clear water. Behind the three boats, unbeknown to us, the logs began to shift and close the gap, meshing together like the teeth of a shark after a meal.

It had been cold but now the sun shone in a clear blue sky and we began to sweat, peeling off layers of anorak and sweater one by one. I felt the RFD shudder violently as an unseen log rammed her, puncturing two hull compartments below the water line. Then the same snag struck the propeller so that the engine leapt into the boat, pulling violently at its transom hinges. Stanley swore as the engine cover struck his wrist, and the boat spun round out of control.

Cutting the engine, we grabbed the oars from their emergency fastening and jabbed hard at the rapidly approaching bank of roots and splintered branches; these were varnished to a shine and razor-sharp through the grinding interaction of the log jam and erosion by winter ice.

My oar blade broke but Stanley managed to steady the cavorting craft until we floated clear from immediate danger.

But we were deep within the jam: sooner or later a log would strike us again and if any further compartments were torn open we would be in grave danger.

I signalled to the other boats. Ben was by himself, for the BBC were filming from the *Forest Engineer*. But he was quick to react and with all his Lifeboat training, handled his boat with skill. Somehow he turned it around as though on a sixpence and skeetered back with precision through the rapidly closing channel. The C-Craft followed at full speed and, being a narrower and altogether smaller boat, almost cleared the jam a few minutes behind Ben. A cluster of floating logs met ahead of them and barred their way but, with the help of Ben's strength from the other side of the jam, they forced a way through to clear water.

Around us the great logs squealed under pressure and all the while the clear strip of water became narrower. Using paddles we strove to retreat back down the corridor until the logs brushed against us on either side and there was still a hundred yards to open water.

The boat began to concertina and the crumpled side edged underneath an encroaching branch. The rubber screeched in shrill protest as the logs closed in about us. There was no future inside the boat so carefully we tested our boots on the slippery surface of the logs.

Not far away the *Forest Engineer*, seeing our plight, had begun to manœuvre backwards and so squeezed the logs against one another. The whole shuddering platform became tightly knit and, though we slithered and fell, our boots found no gaps between the logs.

Desperately we tugged at the old rubber boat. A branch snapped and, with a sudden cork-like splurge, she came free, the logs clashing against each other beneath her like frustrated jaws. There followed an unpleasant journey dragging the boat across a writhing carpet of logs between sharp branches. We were sweating profusely, and not a little frightened by the time we came to a clear patch of water where we slid the boat back into the lake again and had done with our acrobatics.

The *Forest Engineer* emerged and there followed a gloomy journey through the half-drowned forest. The tug led the advance, weaving a slalom course between islands of matted vegetation and the ranks of rotting pine. Sometimes its metal-prowed pontoon would tear through submerged timber with a splintering screech. Dank foliage dripped all over us and hid us from each other. Occasionally clumps of sodden alder, only slightly mashed by the passing screws would spring back into place so we lost the channel. And then, with relief, we reached more open water. There were still floating islands of debris but wide channels lay between them.

On the west bank where the water widened to a great expanse, taking the appearance of an inland sea, we stopped at a group of scruffy cabins built well above the lake. Here a major river flows in from the north-west called the Ingenika. Jack McConnell was over-joyed when he learnt its history from an Indian.

'D'ye hear that,' he shouted, 'Kilroy can take a back seat for

there's noowhere we McConnell's have no been to first, noowhere at
a'. Jim says there's a wee burn away up the Ingenika that is rich in
gold or so it was in 1907 when the first canny McConnell got there
and made his fortune and the burn still bears oor name. What d'ye
say to that, Joe, I dinna recall us passing any Skibinski Mountains
along the way.'

We left Ingenika and thanked Jim Van Somers for the invaluable
aid of his sturdy boat. He warned us to keep to the centre of the lake
where there would be less danger from debris but to head straight
for the nearest shelter if a wind should blow up.

Somewhere, far beneath us, the passing lair of 20-inch Alaska
greyling, lay the grassy flat where Klondiker Collins, foiled by ice
in the fall of 1888, spent the winter and built a trading cabin. The
next year, when the Hudson's Bay Company closed down their port
at Bear Lake, they moved east to Collins' Flat and called their new
store Fort Grahame. It flourished for fifty years but now lies hidden
by many cold green fathoms.

The three boats moved fast, averaging twenty knots, the crews
keeping their eyes skinned for hazards. The larger islands of
flotsam were easy to avoid, but isolated tree trunks—anything from
ten to eighty feet long and almost waterlogged—lay wallowing just
below the surface of the water.

'Go right,' cried the watcher in each craft on seeing a hazard and
the boat would keel violently over as the helmsman wrenched the
tiller aside and throttled down. Perhaps the obstacle had been seen
in the nick of time. If not there would be a violent clunk and the
engine, carefully left in the unlocked position, would leap into the
boat as its shaft collided with the log. A quick inspection to see if all
was well: perhaps a propeller change if necessary and then on
again down the vast expanse of the flooded valley.

A storm blew up as we neared Finlay Forks so we raced at high
speed for shelter. The lake was over five miles wide about here and
the wind quickly whipped up high crested waves which hid all
obstacles. Soon we were soaked through with waves and sleet so
we landed near some old Indian cabins for the night.

Ginnie and her friend Sarah arrived with more fuel supplies, having come by way of the logging road from Mackenzie. They narrowly avoided a swim when they came over a hump and found their road leading straight into the rising lake a few yards ahead.

Searching along the shoreline they found several cabins and, not being sure which was ours, opened the door of the first one and shone their torch around inside. The beam alighted on the totally naked body of a sleeping Indian. One of the girls emitted a dramatic little scream which awoke the Indian who, being annoyed, gave chase without a stitch, followed by the cabin hearthrug which turned out to be a number of fleabitten husky curs.

The girls fled into the night much shaken and I met them later at the office of the enormous timberyard which is the only reason for anyone living at the Forks.

The men work hard and make good pay. A flotilla of tugs towing long rafts of chained logs dump their loads by the factory. The wood is sawn into planking and the waste sawdust and clippings are burnt in two huge incinerators that look like Dutch windmills without arms. By night two roaring pillars of flames show up like beacons throwing clouds of sparks at the moon in an extravagant firework display.

Long after leaving the Forks, we could see the twin blue columns of smoke spiralling against the dark rock of Mount Selwyn, scattering a noxious shower of black ash for miles around. But who is there to worry? Those who suffer immediately from this pollution are only those who make a living from the factory.

It is of course possible to install special equipment to burn the timber waste without releasing harmful residue (provincial legislation to make this compulsory is already under way), but it is expensive and detracts from profits. After all it is a natural temptation for British Columbia's hard-headed business men, whether involved in the mineral, hydrological, or forestry developments, to ruin vast tracts of territory at an alarming but profitable rate in the blissful belief that there is an abundance beyond every horizon.

Great mining complexes are opening up all over beautiful British Columbia to remove for ever a rapidly increasing annual amount of the earth's riches. At the same time played-out mines are closed down after years of work leaving open scars which are seldom covered up.

Later I visited the Bridge River Valley with Ginnie and found a once-scenic region utterly ruined: not so much by the old Bralorne-Pioneer gold mines as by the man-made lakes that have swallowed up the river and much of the valley. No gentle contours, just a series of long rubble-edged reservoirs supported by uninspired walls of concrete. And ragged blotches of broken timber that float forlornly like a scabeous rash over the water. Huge double water-pipes run down the proud face of Seton Valley each broad enough in diameter for a Mini car to drive along. They bring Bridge River water from artificial Carpenter Lake through the bowels of Mission Mountain and down into Seton Lake, 1,200 feet below. A very novel and ingenious hydrological conception which however totally mars the beauty of three great valleys instead of one – which is the normal scenic penalty of an electricity source. Before they were filled with water the tunnels through Mission Mountain were used during the Great Depression by unemployed miners trying to reach the Bralorne mines to find work.

By the fifties, some of the Bralorne mine-shafts were over a mile deep and temperatures became stiflingly hot for the miners. Now the mines are nearly all closed and the towns that rose around them are mostly deserted ghost towns. Nature will quickly cover and reclaim these localised sores for none of the basic organic matter has been removed from the surrounding soil. This is not the case with the enormous open mineral mines which, when exhausted, are often left as unsightly moribund deserts; deserts which spread with the wind and will never again support plant life unless rehabilitated. Stanley Weston, British Columbia's leading expert on soil reclamation, told me it costs 125 dollars an acre to restore fertility in biologically sterile mining waste areas but mining companies are often reluctant to accommodate this sum in their estimates.

In order to stabilise a sterile mined-out area and to prevent further erosion, Mr Weston uses a mulch of straw, sawdust and fibrous materials which protect the newly seeded surface and conserve moisture. Many of the new seeds are of quick-rooting plants which will protect other seeds that root slowly but give a permanent ground cover. A good mixture of seeds will give the necessary diversity of rooting systems – bunch, sod-forming, fibrous and tap-rooting. Alfalfa will put roots down more than forty feet in the soil while the more shallow-rooting grasses will protect the ground completely from the erosive forces of nature.

* * *

From Finlay Forks we bounced south at speed, zipping between bald-headed stakes and floating logs as the lake tapered down to Mackenzie through sixty miles of forest.

An immaculate barge named *The Finlay* intercepted us north of Mackenzie. We were hailed by the skipper, Harry Hanson, chunky ex-Scandinavian and boss of Finlay Navigation whose charter tugs work the lake all round the clock so long as it's ice-free. Ginnie and Sarah were on board and Harry's wife Frankie cooked us a slap-up meal in her poopdeck galley.

The Hansons live in a trailer park, that Canadian phenomenon prevalent in boom towns like Mackenzie which spring up overnight in response to great new industries and where housing is at a premium. Fifteen years ago there was only the forest but the lake has changed all that and now thousands crowd along Mackenzie's spreading miles of tarmac; the workers of the two great timber factories and all the ancillary businesses like Harry's tugs.

The trailers are luxurious inside and the Mackenzie women are known to cook like angels: after all, their men work hard and long all year round making a good fat salary. Harry and Frankie had an office in their trailer and every so often, one or other would rush off to answer the radio telephone: one of the tug pilots was in trouble in a storm and wanted permission to wait out the gale or his log raft might break up . . . two of the men were in jail drunk and were late for an important job . . . Harry rushed off to the Mountie station to bail them out.

We left the Hansons after two days when the boat repairs had hardened and followed the lake south for five miles into an extensive log jam which lay over the old Parsnip River Valley. Narrow and haphazard channels of open water wound between the logs and there seemed no southern river mouth at all.

We nosed deep into the labyrinth of flotsam and kept as close to the southern bank as we might. In the evening between many islands of poplar we found the elusive Pack River, gateway to Summit Lake and thence the Fraser.

Many stories are told of unfortunate travellers who failed to find the Pack River's hidden mouth somewhere along the swampy Flats of Scovil where the giant seven-foot cow parsnips bend their wide white flowers to the river breeze and the Parsnip River pulls hard round to the south-east.

Trappers and prospectors arrived here with the breaking floes of ice, half-starved from bitter winters in the frozen north and hellbent for Fort McLeod where they might find food. If they could locate the Pack they were saved for the Hudson's Bay Company post stood at its source, only seventeen miles upstream at McLeod Lake.

But many missed the tributary including the great sub-Arctic explorer Warburton Pike, who nearly died as a result, and Alexander Mackenzie, who failed to spot the low cutbank which marked the turn-off and so wasted many days following the Parsnip right up to its headwaters and then the Bad River until he finally reached the Fraser not far north of Alexandria.

At first there were no shallows and we rushed smoothly like three grey water ghosts over winding waters sun-dappled through the shrouds of cottonwoods, the gangling grey-white giants that rise without a branch for fifty feet to roofs of delicate foliage. From their trunks were fashioned the long dug-out canoes of the Indians.

The water ran brown and swampy beneath a rotten bridge, after which there were shallows. The long trek had begun. Each day after that, except when we passed through the lakes, there were shallows between every deep pool. A minute or two in the boat perhaps and then the grinding clatter of the propeller against a ledge of rock. Cut the engine, jump out and pull at the lining ropes. After a while another deep stretch. You knew it was deep enough to take the drive-shafts when the icy water was up to your hips. Jump in, tug at the starter cord and—if you're lucky—fifty yards of good going before the next shallow.

And this for sixty miles as the crow flies. Perhaps eighty as the river winds. The Pack was a peaceful, rippling river with no rapids but plenty of fish: rainbow trout, carp and Indian Sapi or bull trout abounded. We also saw fish hawks, ospreys and the rare bald-headed eagle. Every now and again the river widened out into picture postcard lakes which would have been just the place for a tent and a fishing rod with time to spare. Finally we arrived at the river's source in McLeod Lake where there had been a Hudson's Bay Company fort since 1805 and a large Indian population until disease had wiped them out. For fourteen miles we sped along the lake to its southern end into which emptied the dark brown waters of the Crooked River, a fast, shallow and confusing waterway which twisted and turned in a long succession of ox-bow loops and split side channels. For miles we waded, strained and cursed, slithering about in its slippery streambed, pushing and shoving our boats upstream against the flow. At last the river appeared to widen out into a seemingly stagnant slough of quite deep water, so Stanley throttled up, and we thrust past a large red boulder at some twenty knots. There was a shocking clatter, the Evinrude shaft leapt from the water and, on inspection, we found all three propeller blades were missing.

After that we restrained ourselves in patience, for large rocks lay everywhere just below the shiny surface. In places we noticed narrow chutes down which the water ran smoothly like velvet. In these spots all the riverbed boulders had been removed and laid in straight 'lanes' on either side. These were the 'wagon roads' which, legend has it, were made by Twelve-Foot Davis the miner who earned his nickname when he arrived rather late in the day at the Cariboo gold grounds. All the gold-rich areas appeared to have been staked already but Davis, being a crafty little Welshman, spotted a legal loophole which allowed him a twelve-foot long claim between two of the richest stakes in the Cariboo.

He and the other Finlay miners used to bring their winter stores

Traffic duty gloves put to an unusual task on the Crooked River. For seventy winding miles of dwindling river the men strained ten hours a day at the ropes.

Entering the Moran Canyon.

north along the Crooked and it might well have been they who fashioned the 'wagon roads' to speed them on their way downriver.

We camped beside Davie Lake whose shallow marshes abounded with feeding flocks of grebe, geese and loons. Sometimes the water was too shallow even to pull the boats along by line: they would jam on rocks, refusing to budge. Then we would drag them along yard by yard cursing the weight of the 40-horse-power engines which we could seldom use.

For many days we crept wearily south, sometimes despairing of ever reaching Summit Lake, until one day we reached a series of deep pools formed by beaver dams and, later in the evening, spotted the unmistakable hump of Teapot Mountain, northern sentinel of Summit Lake.

In the old days travelling down the Crooked when it flowed too shallow for their riverboats, traders would break up a beaver dam and travel on the brief surge from its released waters until the next dam. This they would break in turn and so reach the Parsnip by courtesy of the beavers' lockgate system. As soon as a boat had gone by the busy beavers would repair the dams.

But going upstream as we were, the dams were awkward obstacles. Once, whilst trying to drag the RFD over a slippery dam wall, Bryn missed his footing, the boat tilted and Stanley fell in as the heavy engine overbalanced on its transom pivot, catching him across the forehead. We fished him out but his eyebrow was deeply cut; blood streamed into his eye and splashed over his stomach. When the wound was cleaned and bound we continued but Stanley's head was throbbing painfully and it was twilight as we passed by Teapot Mountain into Summit Lake and saw a tiny light flashing from the little jetty at the hamlet called Summit Lake.

We had come to the upper limits of the great Arctic watershed, 2,400 feet above sea level. From here the Continental Divide falls east for eleven miles of rolling forest to the Fraser River 200 feet below.

The portage lasted a day following a logging track. Just one of our boats required four porters and, despite the excellence of the track, our necks and shoulders became cramped after a few miles since with three of us being over six feet tall, the boats' fourth corner—supported by little Stanley—was inclined to bounce unevenly.

It seemed a long eleven miles and it was with great relief that we launched the boats on the Fraser late in the afternoon of September 20th. There were over five hundred turbulent miles ahead to the Pacific but the Fraser was deep and the current flowed with us at long last. Two miles downstream lay the Giscome Rapids. For the first time we checked and prepared the emergency air bottles, then we jumped into the boats and the water ripped us away from the bank.

10

The Golden Vein

THE FRASER RIVER FLOWS SOUTH TO THE PACIFIC FOR 850 MILES
in a wide snaking S and we joined it at its most northerly bend. At
first it was deceptively smooth and even the Giscome Narrows were
not as ferocious as we had feared. Here the river showed us its teeth
for the first time, very casually, but menacingly enough to make us
apprehensive. An added hazard was the rash of floating logs on their
way to Prince George and the pulp mills. To many British Colum-
bians, Prince George is the far northern metropolis of their great
province, to us it was back to the world of tarmac and people and a
relaxing of the rules of self-reliance. Now we could expect replenishment from the Land-Rovers at least every third day; sometimes,
when the Fraser ran canyon-free, every evening. It meant less
equipment and fuel to be carried in the boats, and lighter laden we
stood a better chance of survival in the cataracts to come.

Alexander Mackenzie passed by the site of Prince George in 1793
and Simon Fraser, fourteen years later, built a North West Company
fort here. From the fort he plunged south with two dozen experienced canoe men. He was swamped and wrecked, lost canoes,
was threatened by Indians and finally deterred by canyons where the
water dashed against the cliffs and formed great whirlpools, so that
even he dared not continue along the river. Undaunted he found a
way around and finally reached the tidal rivermouth. A latitude star
fix gave him a false position and he turned back two miles before he
reached the true coast.

The Fraser Valley spreads wide and fertile where it bends south at Prince George and is the natural crossing point for traffic from the south and east. The Grand Trunk Pacific Railway arrived here in 1906 after a hard climb over the Rockies. Hundreds died working on the railroad; often of typhoid from the filth and garbage left lying around the advancing tracks. In 1956 a second railway joined Prince George with Vancouver, British Columbia's private Pacific Great Eastern line. Sometimes nicknamed the Prince George Express, it took forty-four years to build which must be some sort of a record.

Between Prince George and Lytton alone, the river drops 1,200 feet, four times the height of the Niagara Falls. Our researches revealed that only one expedition had ever reached Vancouver without much portaging; the expedition of Doctor Elliot Skull from Vancouver whose five-man group had used large inflatable boats. They had written a horrific account of their journey which served as excellent general advice but was little help in detail since the rapids alter both in severity and actual location from year to year and from season to season.

Within the canyons the river rises up to eighty feet at high spring water: then the power of the whirlpools, eddies and hydraulic waves is greater but the danger of hidden rocks causing endless rapids and razor-sharp snares becomes less.

After Giscome Rapids, where the water swirled over confused ridges of submerged rock, we had trouble on the many shifting shingle bars. Twilight came, but we kept on, the dusk intensified by a murky orange smog that stank of rotten garbage larded with a sticky-sweet blend of putrescent fish. The smell of the pulp-mills, say the locals, who live with the odour in their nostrils all year round, is the smell of money. We found the smell repellent and never got used to it, though it was as strong in many other towns to the south.

I shone a torch ahead to spot logs and sandbars. For an age it seemed we slid through the night until, very cold, we came beneath the twin bridges of the town, lit far above us by the pinprick lights of passing cars. Moving with the rolling current, with the engines

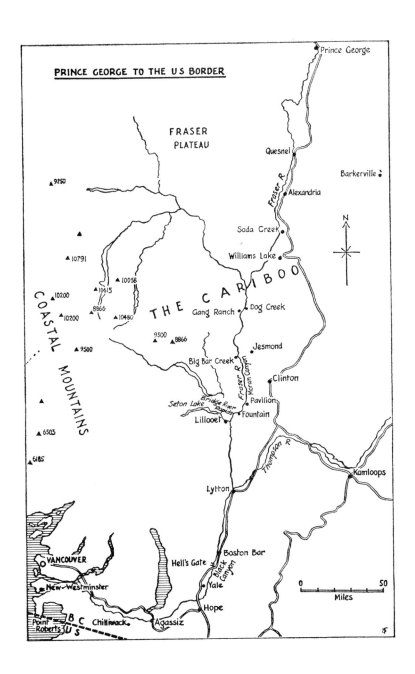

PRINCE GEORGE TO THE U S BORDER

FRASER PLATEAU

▲9250

THE CARIBOO

Prince George

Quesnel

Barkerville •

Fraser R.

Alexandria

Soda Creek •

Williams Lake •

N

▲

▲10791

▲10058

▲10615

▲10200

8866

▲10200

▲10480

Gang Ranch • Dog Creek

9300 8866

▲9500

Jesmond

Big Bar Creek •

Fraser R.

Moran Canyon

Clinton

Bridge River Rapids

Seton Lake

Pavilion

Lillooet •

Fountain

COASTAL MOUNTAINS

▲

▲6505

▲6185

Thompson R.

Kamloops

Lytton

VANCOUVER

New Westminster

Hell's Gate

Black Canyon

Boston Bar

Yale

Hope

0   50

Miles

Point Roberts   B C   Chilliwack   Agassiz

U S

at low throttle, there was a grinding jolt and I shot forward into the bows. We were aground. A moment later the others collided behind us. There was shouting and chaos in the dark but no one was hurt, for we had struck a shelving bank, narrowly missing a line of jagged concrete piles that would have caused much damage to craft and crews. This time we were lucky but I resolved there would be no more travel by night. Carlights flashed from a floatplane jetty and we nosed ashore close to the site of the original Fort George.

The British Trade Commission had arranged an exhibition of our equipment in Prince George's main shopping centre. We stayed in the town for two days as guests of the citizens and received over two hundred orders and enquiries for various items ranging from boats and radios to dehydrated food and flares.

A kindly doctor arranged X-rays and treatment for Stanley and Joe; then we left down the Fort George Canyon, a narrow corridor of contorted rock where the constricted river forges over successive rapids. Just over a hundred years before, the fated Overlanders had come this way with their home-made rafts and frail canoes. Lured from the east of Canada and Britain with exaggerated tales of gold and an easy life promised by the British Columbia Overland Transit Company, these amateur miners travelled 3,000 miles to reach the Cariboo. The Fraser drove many to desperate ends; its sandbars were littered with the skeletons of rafts and canoes as well as the broken bodies of the Overlanders. One group of five men were wrecked in a canyon. Two managed to reach Fort George before it was cut off by winter snow. The other three were found the following spring. Official records have kept their names a secret but their pitiful story is widely known. Driven to extremes of cold and hunger, two of them killed their partner and ate him. Later there was a second murder and the surviving cannibal was eventually killed by Indians in whose possession some of his belongings were found.

The Fraser appeared to be used as an easy open sewer for untreated chemical waste from the mills. We could no longer safely drink the river water without first boiling and sterilising it. I tasted some later and regretted it, for it was nauseous, although not as powerfully so as Thames water. Rusty piles of abandoned cars had been dumped along the banks by Quesnel and detergent spun in blobs of floating mud-flecked scum and dead fish circled, belly upward in the eddies.

Quesnel was the northern Fraser terminus of an interesting failure in 1866, when the Western Union Telegraph Company established a telephone line from New Westminster that was part of a proposed link-up from Western Europe through Siberia, Alaska and British Columbia to America. Using mules and Chinese labour the British Columbia stretch was completed in two summers and the first message transmitted from the US told of Abraham Lincoln's assassination. This was also just about the last message because, only a year later, a telephone cable was successfully laid beneath the Atlantic.

In 1858 a Cornish potter called Billy Barker became a sailor and jumped his ship to join the Fraser gold rush. After four years of digging, he struck Cariboo gold. His lucky shaft had already gone down forty feet in vain. When does a man give up? At forty-two feet he struck it rich.

The news spread and Barkerville sprang up. In no time at all it was the largest town north of San Francisco and west of Chicago. Destroyed by fire one day, it was rebuilt in a week. Values got out of hand as the place flourished. At one time a dance with a hotel girl cost ten dollars and any further favours considerably more. The patriarch, Billy Barker, married one of the local girls and spent his fortune only to die in an old folks' home without a penny. But he must have lived it up for quite a while for he and his partners took 600,000 dollars of pay dirt from their claim. By the turn of the century Barkerville was a shambling ghost town with no more golden eggs to lay.

As far south as Quesnel and Barkerville, the Fraser runs at almost the same level as the land: to the south it flows within a deep trough valley many hundreds of feet below the surface of the surrounding landmass. The river responds to the new resistance of the enclosing walls by seeking a sinuous route through an endless succession of nightmarish canyons, livid with angry foam, mad with the roar of boiling water echoing upwards to the exclusion of all other sound.

Not knowing what lay around each tortuous curve we grew increasingly nervous as the days went by and the cataracts grew more powerful and more frequent. In a small rubber boat even a twelve-foot wave can seem fatally high. When they are many and come from everywhere and move from side to side with speed to disappear in the gurgling maw of whirlpools, then they bring fear. The more so when each man knows that the Impossible cataract or Bottomless whirlpool of his nightmares may well lie around the next corner or the next or the next.

The maps were no good; they could not hope to be, for the rapids change year by year. They clearly showed a place called the Iron Rapids. After a seventy-mile stretch of recurrent rough water through deep curling canyons we finally reached the supposed locations of these rapids and the spot was as calm as a millpond, relatively speaking. Elsewhere we moved through long corridors and bottlenecks where the boats were hidden one from the other in a welter of high dashing waves. Though the motors proved powerless against the violent undercurrents, the craft took the successive batterings and swamping with little damage and minimal loss of equipment. It was not evident at the time but the unrelenting canyon and the nameless fear it stirred within us was causing invisible damage to morale.

South of Quesnel, in calmer waters, scurries of perky sandpipers ran along the shinglebars uttering high forlorn cries most unsuited to such cheerful birds. There were kingfishers too, larger than I had seen before and one evening I watched a little red squirrel swim away from the bank and out into the river until some two hundred yards away it disappeared from sight. I hoped fervently that it reached the other bank whatever its thieving mission. I had a ridiculous, almost superstitious desire to see nothing drown in the Fraser.

The region was rich in porcupines and skunks though I saw only one of these black and white beauties at close quarters and froze with respect until it passed me by. An Indian in the Cariboo told me that the pretty white-striped skunks can throw their 'smell' at least eight feet. They just point their backside at anything or anyone that bothers them and a fine yellowish spray is propelled as though from an aerosol. The resulting odour lasts for a very long time and renders the victim as undesirable as a leper. Live skunks make very clean and un-smelly pets whether or not their scent-glands are removed; indeed they can be house-trained far more quickly than most poodles. But run one over and it will have the last laugh for your car will stink for many a day.

During the anxious days before we came to the Moran Canyon, Bryn often travelled in the BBC boat for photographic reasons and I came to know Stanley quite well. Most of our time was taken up concentrating on staying alive, choosing the correct channel through the great rapids, avoiding rocks and whirlpools. Moving at twenty-five knots as we were, this required total attention on the water ahead. But there were calmer reaches where we could enjoy the scenery, the deserted gold seekers' shacks and slatted flumes along the narrow shingle beaches. The whole vast land seemed deserted save for some cattle and free-range horses, and once two shaggy men who stood and stared from a ghost hamlet. One of them shouted and moved down towards the river. He seemed to be pointing ahead and mouthing a warning that was whipped away by the roar of the river. He moved in stiff-gaited hops like a frog. He had no stick to help him and I saw that one leg was missing from the thigh: his strength and balance must have been remarkable. We were swept past the cripple into a great canyon. I noticed that rapids called Frenchman's Bar were indicated some miles further within the canyon. Remembering the so-called Iron Rapids, I paid little heed.

Five ruined shacks clustered by the gaping cavern of a long-dead mine shaft. Those huts told a sorry tale that we heard much later. Four years before, an American from Seattle had bought up the mine and arrived at Big Bar Ferry, eight miles downriver, with an 18-foot riverboat powered by twin 50-horse-power engines. Leaving his car at the ferry he launched the boat and set out in fine style with his nineteen-year-old son and a friend who'd come to see the mine. Somewhere just below the shacks the Americans were swamped by a rapid, their friend drowned at once, and they clung to the upturned boat which was swept down to the mouth of the

Moran Canyon. A chance eddy threw the craft against a sandbar and the young man pulled his unconscious father ashore before making his way to the ferry cabin for help. Five hours later his father was carried to shelter and warmth but by then his hands and legs were badly frozen. Gangrene had set in and both his legs had to be amputated. Neither father nor son ever went back to their mine by the five old shacks.

The area of rolling plains around and above us was called the Cariboo: it was another world way over our heads and its sagebrush meadows were dusted with the first fine layer of winter snow. Far below, in the Cariboo's 'basement', we were permanently cold despite thick sweaters and anoraks, for the rapids soaked us through. We talked to keep our minds warm. Stanley was less reticent than usual about his past. He was, he admitted, nervous of what lay ahead for he was engaged to be married and had seen a lot of death during his army years. In Cyprus early in 1963, Stanley's patrol had watched the cars of Cypriots ambushed and shot up. They had been unable to intervene but, when it was over, they had dragged the bodies clear. It had been unpleasant: Stanley remembered feeling sick and helpless. Later he had been trained as a medic, after which on such occasions, he had still felt sick but no longer helpless. They had been badly ambushed in the Trudos Mountains. Afterwards in Dar-es-Salaam and Germany, Stanley had become a first-grade mechanic and machinist and worked for a year in the stifling heat of the Bahrein workshops. He was in Aden next, where British soldiers were in season for both guerrilla factions. The Crater district exploded and Stanley's unit were soon at work sealing coffins: those available were the regulation size of five feet eight inches but many of the corpses were over six feet. The heat was great; there could be no decent waiting for longer coffins but it was not a pleasant job having to break legs or ankles with a rope in order to seal the lids.

On a day off, Stanley was sunbathing outside his quarters at Khormaksar with some friends. There was a clatter of feet outside the wire fence, a dark shadow whipped briefly across the compound and then an exploding flash. Stanley felt only the shock and a numbing pain in his arm, torn open by shrapnel. Three soldiers lay writhing close by. One died quickly; the others were horribly mutilated.

Stanley was pleased to leave Aden.

Once on leave from Germany, he scrounged a free lift to Washington with Lufthansa. In 1886 the British troops had burnt down the White House when the Americans had dared to rebel against His Britannic Majesty but our Redcoats, being mostly Prussian mercenaries, had not been thorough, according to Stanley because a six foot by four portrait of the arch-villain himself, George Washington, had been saved by the rebels and now reclined at the new White House.

Determined to finish off the job properly on behalf of the Queen, our Stanley befriended an official from the Pentagon and obtained a guided tour of the White House as well as an interview with Mr Nixon. All went well until he was caught red-handed with his petrol lighter at full blast on Mr Washington's frock coat. Unfortunately the President was not very inflammable and the imperialistic Cribbet was speedily removed with his lion's tail tucked between his legs.

*   *   *

We moved at twenty-five knots through the canyon. Ahead the ravine opened up and the river was 500 yards in width. But not for long: half a mile further on the black walls closed in again to form a narrow bottleneck which the map called Frenchman's Bar Rapids.

Being keyed up to expect the worst at the distant narrows, I failed to pay much attention to the water dead ahead until too late. Suddenly Stanley throttled down and the engine idled. There was no noticeable decrease in our speed and a new sound took over from the high thrum of the engine. Where the Fraser began to close in towards the narrows a sinister line of white horses showed right across the river: the lip of a waterfall.

There was little enough time to think. The main thing is always to look for the V, that dark smooth chute of water that cannons between the rocks of a cataract. However violent the crash of water against rock to either side of the V, the chute itself is safe enough until it drops down into the turbulence below, where the greatest hydraulics and whirlpools are to be found. In short, a V-chute will lead a boat down through the roughest region of any rapid but also through the only rock-free area.

Standing up in the bows, I scanned the foaming lip that rushed towards us and sighted the telltale dark patch over to our right. I shouted to Stan whose vision ahead was impeded by the rise of our bows and pointed towards the V.

Applying full throttle we headed diagonally across the river aiming directly for the V, our only hope, since it was already obvious—by the deep volume of sound and the bouncing welter of spray thrown up beyond the cataract—that this would be far worse than anything we had yet experienced. We moved broadside on towards the foaming ledge and still were not quite far enough over to make the V. I screamed back at Stanley to straighten out, for it seemed too late now to gain the V-chute. At least we should enter the rocky vortex bows-on. I prayed briefly and gripped the safety line. This was it.

But Stanley had not heard my yell which was whipped away as it left my mouth. He kept on towards the V and the bows nudged its racing chute as we shot over the very brink of the cataract. The old boat reared over sideways and I gasped in horror as I saw the pounding water drop away beneath us to the foaming maw below.

It seemed as though we hung for a moment with our bows caught by the V-chute and the stern over the deadly rock jaws below. Then the sheer speed of the chute sucked us over the ledge and down into the heart of a giant hydraulic. For a moment we were underwater and then rising, rising as on the crest of a tidal wave. The engine raced at full power and the screw threshed against the backwash of the comber that held us and sucked backwards to bury us under the cataract. The engine won and a second wave spewed us clear into the lesser chaos below.

The other boats had watched our desperate race across the face of the cataract and both moved over to the correct course in good time. When we disappeared from view they could not know how we fared but, like us, they had no alternative and both survived the backwash.

Looking back we realised there could have been no chance at all of survival had we passed over the cataract at any point either side of the chute. I looked at Stanley. He grinned wickedly as he watched me tip back my crash helmet to wipe the sweat and spray from my forehead.

Seven miles downriver was a low bank called Big Bar where an old cable ferry takes the occasional tourist over the river. A lonely ferryman lives close by. The place is desolate enough and is the last stopping place before the terrible canyons of Moran. Once committed to their forty-mile corridors there could be no turning back.

I had no reliable information about the Moran and it would be suicide to enter the canyon without some form of reconnaissance.

*   *   *

The Land-Rovers were not at Big Bar awaiting us as expected. But a large Canadian with a white woolly sweater and spectacles arrived in a Ford Pickup and introduced himself as Malcolm Turnbull, the City Editor of the Vancouver Province newspaper. They had been reporting the expedition's progress almost as closely as had their opponents, the *Sun* and, after their initially cynical attitude, had become temporarily quite friendly.

The nearest Cariboo town where we might find information about the Moran was Clinton, two hours' drive to the east. Malcolm took the men to lodgings there, Joe stayed with the ferrykeeper to guard the boats and I waited at Big Bar for the Land-Rovers.

They never came. After four hours I began to worry. They had over a hundred miles of vertiginous roads to drive in order to meet us. The night before, we had camped by an old gold mine near Riske Creek and the girls had met us there. Both were towing the heavy trailers in addition to fully-laden rear compartments and roof racks. It is difficult to reverse with trailers attached and the girls were not strong enough to detach the coupling hooks themselves. Sarah's machine was new but Ginnie's was prehistoric and we never ceased to wonder how it kept going.

Its battery troubles had finally been resolved in Mackenzie.

Ginnie had arrived there one morning after a long drive from Fort Nelson. Leaving the vehicle in the car park outside the police station, she got out and was about to slam the door when the battery exploded and the entire wiring system caught fire.

Clouds of smoke everywhere and lots of men running about, three with fire extinguishers.

A Mountie, the car park attendant, and a man from the Fire Department argued vehemently as to who should use their extinguisher. Eventually the Mountie suggested disconnecting the batteries which were flame-free. This did the trick and an extremely kind constable called Corporal Thompson spent eight hours rewiring the ignition system alone. From then on Ginnie had only been able to start by touching a wire from the battery against the solenoid.

Afterwards the brakes had ceased to function and a rear half-shaft and the universal joint had broken: the vehicle's age was beginning to tell. All this and numerous minor defects did not make for happy motoring along the dizzy roads and tracks which the girls had to follow to keep us resupplied.

I hitched a lift on a farm lorry to the main track crossing by Jesmond Ranch and at dusk the girls arrived—separately and from different directions. Both were as mud-bespattered as their vehicles.

They had a tale of woe to explain their lateness which included getting lost in a strange desert region by Gang Ranch, breaking down on a teetering bridge with rotten and partially missing planking, and having to change a wheel on a hairpin bend by Dog Creek (many miles away from the correct route). At some stage Sarah had skidded into a deep flood ditch from which Ginnie had finally towed her after many abortive attempts. A duststorm and later a snowstorm had not helped matters. Passing through the scenic Farrell Canyon of the Chilcotin River both girls swore they had seen many tall storks; black and white with baggy bills. When I suggested they had been delivering babies to the outlying ranchers, the girls were not amused.

*　*　*

On a fruitless search for an informant about Moran waters we visited Williams Lake, well north of Clinton and deep into the Cariboo; it was just a hamlet along the old fur-trading route until the gold rush when prospector William Dietz struck lucky and soon fifty million dollars' worth of gold had been taken from the land. Now the place is a thriving centre to the cattle ranches of the Cariboo rangeland which stretches like an oval saucer with the Fraser a deep crack down its centre. A hundred and sixty miles long and nearly as wide it is confined by the western Coastal Range and the Rockies to the east. The Thompson River shapes its southern limits and, to the north, the high sources of the Arctic watershed. It is good ranching land—over four thousand feet above sea level—rich in fine meadows and upland lakes: too dry an area for dairy farming but excellent for beef cattle. Wild horses once roamed the country but a bounty was announced and they were slaughtered in thousands. Most of it is too dry and remote to be commercially viable for mixed farming, but in the Lower Fraser Valley, south and west of Chilli- wack, farmers have a ready market in Vancouver so the country supports vegetable and dairy farms in the fertile regions and egg or broiler poultry farms in the hills. Grain farming is more or less restricted to the Peace River district and fruit farming to the Okanagan Valley where apples, peaches and apricots, pears, plums, cherries and even grapes are grown.

Down by Big Bar, the Fraser canyon has its own little micro- climate but the sheer-sided fields of dry sagebrush and tumbleweed only need a little water to produce fine crops. I saw whole acres of green sprouting beneath a wide network of revolving sprinklers; the water supply coming from an upland lake by gravity. The small amount of farming that is done still amounts to British Columbia's largest consumptive water requirement but that matters little because over a third of all Canada's rainwater flows within British Columbia. Even the Americans cast envious eyes north to the vast reservoir of the Rocky Mountain Trench as an answer to the pro- blems of their dry western belt, until the Columbia River was dammed.

The Cariboo has settled down to quiet farming since its goldrush days. Even then there was little trouble; a few minor murders of and by hostile Indians, and a quickly muted rebellion by badman Ned McGowan. The famous 'hanging judge' Matthew Begbie established a threadbare but effective constabulary without difficulty, for there was too much work and too many problems even getting from A to B; leaving little time for skulduggery. Horses or mules were the only means of transport along the perilous route of the Old Cariboo Trail until it was widened to take wagons. An exception were the imported camels which a shrewd freighter named Frank Laumeister set to work at cut-rate prices carrying three times the amount as the same number of mules.

Unfortunately every time a heavy-laden mule train met up with the camels, they became panicstricken at the sight and smell of the ungainly beasts and fled – often over the edge of the precipice to free-fall into the Fraser far below. Indignant muleteers, with embryonic inklings of trades unionism, objected as much to the camels as present-day dockers to containers. A flurry of lawsuits for damages soon had Laumeister withdrawing his poor creatures, which he abandoned along the Thompson flats where they became extinct in 1905.

When the Cariboo gold ran out, only a handful of miners stayed to ranch. They needed wives so they ordered suitable women from the Bishop of Oxford in Britain who sent out five dozen post-haste; all were married within days of arrival in the Cariboo and proved very robust. Since then Oxford has changed to exporting Austin and Morris cars which are equally reliable.

For three days, based at Clinton, we tried to reconnoitre the Moran Canyon.

Helicopters and aeroplanes were unobtainable without expensive hire charges. Specially prepared aerial photos were being prepared by the British Defence Liaison Staff in Ottawa but would not arrive for a week – which was too long to wait.

We drove over the magnificent hump of Pavilion Mountain to the southern end of the canyon, and found an old ferry trail down to the river. Looking up the river with binoculars we could see no more than a mile or so which included two long rough stretches. It was

Above Hell's Gate and below

The old silver boat strains to escape back-suction below a chute on the Fraser—without success.

impossible to see more and pointless to struggle along the rugged canyons in the hope of a better view further north since the canyon walls were thousands of feet high and so acutely angled that a grandstand view from the very rim of the cliffs would probably not allow a glimpse of the river itself.

Driving down to the Indian reservation at Pavilion we paid our respects to the Chief who said that, not being crazy, he had never been in the Moran Canyon nor would ten thousand spirits drive him there. However he directed us to the chicken-clucking, cur-yapping, papoose-yowling abode of a blind old man who had once been Chief many moons back in the days when there was a manned railway station along the cliffs somewhere up the canyon. He couldn't say exactly how to get there, nor could he think of anyone else who would know. Such folk would all be dead just as he soon would be, God willing. But he did know that many many Indians and white men had died in the 'great canyon' over the years. No one with any sense entered the place. We would do well to avoid it. Folk used to say the canyon waters were haunted by evil spirits, that there were waves so high that even a metal steamboat of the whites was dashed to pieces, that there were whirlpools which stretch across the entire width of the river.

The old man was all set to dwell further on the pleasures of river travel in the canyon beside which he had been brought up and lived ever since but, before he could put us off completely, we bade him good day and drove north the very next day to Big Bar to try our luck at the northern end of the hidden canyon.

Here the Fraser bushland shelves in wild seclusion between the upper forests, leading steep and inaccessible to the higher plateaux, and the actual cliffs enclosing the river. A dusty farm trail wound along the bench between scraggy cornfields and from time to time led us close to the gorge. After twelve miles the trail swung away from the river at 'Ed's Ranch', a ramshackle building straight from a Charles Adams cartoon or a Hitchcock scenario. The place seemed deserted and we clambered over a broken fence to walk down to the canyon.

Someone shouted from an outhouse. A tough-looking fellow in

denims, face pocked and hair cropped Buddhist-wise, confronted us with a scowl.

'That's where the track goes,' he grunted, pointing inland to Kelly Mountain. 'This here's ma land and ah don't encourage no strangers, see.'

I hastened to reassure him that we only wished to view the river. Perhaps we could take a photograph of him by his farm with the wide backdrop of the Fraser Canyon.

'Oh. No, you don't take no pictures of me, fellah, nor the house. And if you wanna see the river, you jist cross them cornfields. There ain't no need to mosey around here, see. What d'you want with the river anyway? You won't catch fish 'cos you can't nowise get down them cliffs.'

A Land-Rover cab and part of its chassis, buckled almost beyond recognition, lay derelict in the farmyard, sheltering a beautifully worked mid-western saddle.

He saw me looking at the old machine and gave a humourless chuckle.

'The trail hairpins up them cliffs at an angle you gotta see to believe,' he said, indicating the sheer forest slopes to the east. 'Ah was drivin' her down one day last yeer and a tyre burst. Over the edge we went a rollin' and a bouncin' fer hundreds of yards till she fetched up agin a tree. And that's all that's left of her. More's the shame 'cos she was the best wagon Ah ever had.'

He seemed to warm to us a bit, giving Ginnie an appraising look with his intensely cold blue eyes.

He said he'd show us a way to the edge of the canyon from where we could see the Fraser. He climbed into our Land-Rover and, following his directions, we jolted through meadows, along storm gulleys, until the country became too steep and we walked through knee-high poppies to the very edge of the dizzy gorge. The cavernous roar of the river came to us from far below in the black abyss, and Ginnie recoiled instinctively.

Just behind us our guide laughed softly.

'About four years ago,' he said, 'at this time of the year, when the water's gettin' so cold you'd freeze in minutes if you didn't drown

194

first, Ah was workin' in this very field and Ah heerd someone a screamin'. Whoever it is, Ah remember thinkin', he's in terror fer his life. Ah could tell by the way his heart was put into them cries. And the echoes of 'em kept a ringin' outa the canyon. Right heer it was. 'Course by the time I came and had a look, there was nothin' down there but the screams a-chasin' one another round the rocks. Kinda strange it was, seein' as nothin' could survive in the river. Wicked water is the Moran.'

We left that eerie spot and took our guide back to his farmhouse. He was still standing watching us as we bucked round a distant bend and drove down the narrow trail to Kelly Creek.

We came to the shack of an old fellow named Andy Moses. He said he'd lived in the valley all his life but he knew nothing about the river within the Moran.

'Never been down there,' he drawled. 'Too many guys drowned in the canyon. Anybody who tries to boat through's just plumb crazy.'

A few miles further on we were back at Big Bar. Joe was drinking coffee with Joe Bishop, the kindly old ferry hand. He had just come back from the far bank by ferry after visiting a small colony of hippies who lived in an old miner's shack. They grew marijuana and all their own vegetables.

Even Joe Bishop who had always lived at Big Bar knew next to nothing about Moran waters but he told us of two young Albertan canoeists who were making a film of their journey from Fort St James to Vancouver. Both men were expert slalom canoeists using a 14-foot craft and the best in lifesaving equipment.

He had watched them arrive from Gang Ranch Bridge: each of them used the canoe on alternate days whilst the other drove the car to the next prearranged meeting point. After their change-over at Boston Bar, the car-driver for that day had waved his friend goodbye into the Moran and driven south to Lillooet. Two days later, his friend had not arrived so he arranged a helicopter search. They found the body floating round and round in an eddy somewhere in the Moran Canyon: the dead man's expertise had proved inadequate.

These tales of death and many others were not encouraging. We had been at Clinton for three days and the signs were growing that the men's morale would crack up unless we made a move. I was not at all keen to enter the canyon where so many had drowned without prior knowledge of the dangers involved but now there was nothing for it. Caution must be thrown to the winds for any further waiting would seriously affect the ability of the men to face whatever hazards might be ahead.

As we left Big Bar Creek, Joe Bishop had a last message of comfort.

'Whatever the rapids in the canyons are like, lads, they won't be as murderous as Hell's Gate. That's fer sure 'cos I've seen it. Good luck to you.'

Soon Big Bar was but a memory and the canyon walls, over a thousand feet high, grey black and shiny, rose above us sheer from the water. Bars and shingle banks were few and far between. The current gathered momentum mile by mile and soon the great river fought through a deep curving gut no more than fifteen yards wide. The resulting underplay of cross-currents was immense and irresistible.

Stanley would shake his head in disbelief as the boat shot sideways, even turned about completely in the grip of huge boils which erupted beneath us and tore us away from our chosen course. It was unnerving. The underlying fear – of what new chaos lurked round each successive bend – crept clammily around our spines and tightened our bowels. We crouched in silence, fighting to keep away from the powerful suction currents of the jagged cliffs with their cavernous overhangs.

Time passed by unnoticed, as did the miles. Our ears became accustomed to the overbearing all-pervading noise of the churning water. From time to time I fiddled nervously with the screw-tap of my air-bottle, checking its position with sweating fingers. But we came through the cataracts, skirted the greedy whirlpools and three times managed to land upriver of especially evil water to reconnoitre a route through.

Later in the evening the railway cabin of Fountain station peeped down at us a mile or two above the great killer-rapid of the Bridge River confluence. We made for the bank with speed and pulled the boats ashore before climbing the long steep slope to the road 600 feet above the river.

A nation-wide controversy is now raging around the Moran Canyon where a 750-foot dam is planned that would form a lake stretching right up the spine of the Cariboo. If the dam is built it will destroy the greatest Sockeye* salmon river in the world and the richest delta in Canada. The undammed Fraser brings silt, rich in nutrients, to its wide estuary so that it hums with life—being far more productive of living organisms than the open sea. From every upland tributary of the Fraser the young salmon swim south to this delta and the sea to feed. When mature, usually four years later, they return to the gravel stream of their birth to spawn. This done, they die, for they eat nothing during their journey from the sea and receive a severe battering against rocks as they fight through successive rapids and falls.

Water pollution is already affecting the salmon industry: to dam the Fraser will very quickly kill off this unique and self-perpetuating natural resource which annually accrues over a hundred million dollars for the province. One man-made factor which fortunately augurs against the damming of the Fraser is that the country's three rail companies all use lines that cut along the canyon walls not far above the present-day highwater mark. When the railways were built, large-scale dumping of rock and unexpected landslides blocked up much of the narrow canyon called Hell's Gate so that the water rushed through the bottleneck at up to fifty miles an hour and the salmon could no longer reach their spawning grounds. Specially constructed fish ladders which bypass the maelstrom and so allow the fish upriver access were built in 1945 but the Sockeye had still not recovered to their earlier numbers estimated at the time of the 1913 landslides. This is tangible evidence of the disruption any dam will cause the Fraser salmon cycle.

* * *

*The Sockeye or Alaskan Red Salmon averages 28 inches and 7 lbs. The Chinook or Spring Salmon averages 38 inches and 25 lbs. (maximum known was 80 lbs.) Other varieties of Fraser salmon are the Humpback, Chum and Coho.

We passed a merry evening at the home of eighty-five-year-old Ma Murray, Queen of Lillooet and famous through Canada as the rumbunctious, irascible, but likable old-timer who personifies the pioneering spirit of British Columbia. In particular she pioneered newspapers and still runs the very personalised *Bridge River News* — on the front page of which is written in large letters 'Circulation — 1572 copies and Every Bloody One Paid For!'

At Lillooet the Fraser begins to cut its way into the Coastal Mountains and the town lies low, protected by mountains in a wide and scenic valley where sunshine predominates, rainfall is rare, winters mild, and summers hot and dry. Sick people who would die elsewhere live on happily at Lillooet to flourish alongside fields of tropical fruit and vegetables. Even grapes grow well with a sugar content higher than that of California.

The river flows beneath the great bridge at Lillooet in wide fluctuating eddies, the aftermath of the cataract at the Bridge River junction. When we arrived at Lillooet, Ma Murray was ill in hospital and her kindly daughter Georgie looked after us, keeping our minds off the Bridge River Rapids.

After Lillooet's heyday had passed by with its gold supply, ranching and big-game hunting had taken over. Each self-respecting town in the area held an annual rodeo; usually as parochial as an English village gymkhana. We watched the Lillooet rodeo, held just outside the town in a flat dusty basin. The audience cluttered around the outer corral cheering the contestants, though few of them were locals; mostly professional cowboys who travel the country from rodeo to rodeo and show great expertise. The dust flew high and little Indian kids grew apoplectic with excitement so that they fell into the arena until grabbed away by Mum's firm hand. There were competitions of calf-trussing, bull-riding, bronco-busting and cow-roping; all the traditional skills of the Wild West ranches.

Many of the audience were Indians of the Lillooet tribe; a happy boisterous people mostly clad in après-roundup clothing. Only four generations ago, the men from this same tribe of the 'Skumakum' or 'land of plenty' were the Indians described in James Teit's book of 1906 which tells of the great battles between the Lillooet and

Chilcotin Indians. On one occasion some Lillooets found a squaw in tears and accompanied her back to her village which had been raided. The occupants had all been killed, the children disembowelled and their bodies impaled on sticks. The Lillooets immediately visited their opponents for a return match and scored a bloody victory. Such was life in the days before the 'Wahnitu' arrived, the new white tribes who outlawed wars and feuds in all the land but back in their home countries killed each other in millions not hundreds.

* * *

Reaction had set in after the tension of the preceding weeks. We knew the rubber boats were not invincible; Cranberry Rapids had proved that, and now we had our first glimpse of the Bridge River Rapids. The sight was not encouraging nor was the sound which we began to hear a mile away from the cataract, but for me the complete mastery of such water over everything that came within its thrall posed a compelling challenge. Some see a mountain slope and cannot wait until they're dangling from its cliffs. Others drool over ocean charts and long to feel the pounding seas about them in some frail but trusty ketch. Thousands respond to the thrill of paperwork expeditions with technical or financial objectives where an error of judgment can spell disaster and unpredictable risks abound. These are the 'paper tigers' whose pith helmets are bowler hats, their maps are pink newspapers, and their rifles, umbrellas. Their base is deep within the commuter belt and they daily risk contagion travelling through the human jungle, often by subterranean routes, to their various research stations.

Just above the Bridge River's mouth, the river winds through the shelving gash of Fountain Ravine, foaming over a series of rapids, and jinks sharply south to boil furiously, at thirty-five knots, over a ledge of serrated rock. The water is chaotic; huge spiralling waves rise snake-like from the seething surface of the maelstrom and explode one upon the other in a fury of spray. Great bottomless whirlpools whisk logs into their maw and swallow them whole whilst convoluting boils, over six feet high, rush sideways into dark caverns cut into the black cliffs that rim both banks. The shattering boom of the cataract echoes out along the valley and, watching, we could feel our tails wither, and tuck themselves dejectedly between our legs. We had been over many rapids but this was surely unthinkable; certain suicide.

The word had spread to Vancouver whose reporters, photographers and television men had gathered, like vultures brimming with anticipation, and were setting up their vantage points on the more accessible western bank where the concrete corridors of a fish ladder fringed the river.

Watching the behaviour pattern of the cataract, I noticed that logs sucked down by the whirlpools were spewed up some hundreds of yards downriver after an immersion of about two minutes. A lifejacketed body, though equally buoyant, would be a smaller and easier morsal for the suction currents and so might well suffer a far longer period beneath the water. A grain of comfort were our special breather-bottles, supposed to contain some four minutes of air for use in an emergency.

I re-read the instructions sent with the bottles. They were carefully worded by the Technical Officer of the unit responsible:

To Army Strategic Command—You will appreciate that the breathing sets have been made up to suit the peculiar requirements of Exercise Headless Valley and do not constitute officially recognised equipment. Trials carried out by this Branch have proved that the minimum breathing period could be limited to one minute in conditions of maximum physical effort . . . This Branch will not accept responsibility in the event of an accident.

An onlooker who lived in Lillooet but had come from Britain a few years before told me that some months earlier he had met a very muscular Frenchman whose prowess as a slalom canoeist was well known. He had canoed every major rapid in North America including the great Lava sinkholes of the Colorado and had come to tame the Bridge River Rapids. His battered body was retrieved below the whirlpools soon after he entered the cataract and ended up on a cold hospital slab.

It took quite a while to descend the steep cliff to the boats. I slipped on a wet boulder and one foot landed on a jagged rock which slit through the rubber of my gym shoe and cut the sole of my foot open causing a wide gash an inch deep. I limped down to the boats far below leaving a trail of blood. There was a first aid kit in the boats and Paul Berriff bound the foot with expertise. The bandage was soon soaked through but I squeezed the foot into a black rubber 'frog-shoe' in which the blood squelched about alarmingly but the wound was protected.

We navigated four rapids successfully in the gorge below Fountain but nerves were strained to breaking point and at the fourth rapid, a single high standing wave, matters came to a head.

The little C-Craft was more prone to capsize than the larger RFDs and the crew had already had narrow escapes over the first three rapids. They were now unwilling to take the boat through the fourth hazard, knowing that a capsize there would involve the possibility of being swept over the great cataract just around the bend.

There was no point in forcing anyone to continue against their will, so the C-Craft was lined through the rapid.

Beyond it, our mouths dry with apprehension we swept around the wide shoulder of the Fountain Ravine. Fighting the tremendous suction of the millrace we rammed the rocks above the upper lips of the cataract and fastened the bowlines to boulders.

Limping along the rocks, I saw that 400 yards upriver of the main turmoil a rock ledge ran right across the river and churned the water into a single foaming channel beset with broken rock. Should a boat capsize here there would be no time to re-right it. In a minute it would be swept over the waterfall below.

Bryn and the BBC set up their filming points whilst the rest of us studied the water. Stanley and I would take the silver boat through followed by the Scotsmen in the BBC's black RFD. All being well the little C-Craft would then be cast loose unmanned to make its own way downriver. This was the plan.

The sun shone close. I felt drained of energy and faint. The rubber suits were warm and clammy. I saw the hot rock glistening red and noticed that my frog-boot was leaking blood. A growing hum invaded my skull; the glare from the river was intense. I lay in an eddy clinging to a rock as the water rose and fell violently in the backwash from the turbulence. Gloriously cool water seeped through into the frog-suit, splashed over my face and crash helmet, and I felt better. We MUST go now. The temptation to wait and discuss routes was strong. My stomach fluttered wildly; Stanley shivered despite the heat and his long face was pallid. He ground out a cigarette weakly on a rock.

From a high boulder downriver Richard Robinson gave us the signal and Stanley whipped our engine into life. Plucked from the bank like a cork we ran through the white water below the first rock ledge. Twice the propeller ground violently against submerged rocks and we scarcely dared breathe as the engine burred unevenly, threatening to stall. If it did, there would be perhaps thirty seconds in which to re-start it or man the emergency oars before reaching the main waterfall.

But the engine remembered the Nahanni and the Liard, the Kechika and the Crooked and did not fail us. The rocks were behind and now a short stretch of smooth racing water, too powerful to fight against, sucking us straight into the maw of the cataract.

I glanced back at Stanley. He was testing the valve control of his air-bottle, the knuckles of his tiller hand white as he forced us away from the cliff.

A roar like the thunder of doom stirred ahead as we raced powerless into the heart of sound. For a while we could see nothing until, at the brink of the great foaming chute, a scene of incredible turmoil seethed below us. As if entering hell we slid down the boiling flume to be engulfed by a huge hydraulic within which we cork-screwed deeper and deeper. We could see nothing but foam, being awash and moving within a tunnel of cartwheeling water that closed over our heads. The whole boat keeled over, forced up the side of the monster wave by centrifugal force. It was a wall of death on the vertical plane and our hull clung to the moving wave although we had tipped over at an acute angle. We were almost upside down within that whirling tunnel, only able to see a confused kaleidoscope of surging water, and numbed by the overall din.

At the nadir of the hydraulic's cyclic action, the undertow caught us, dragging the boat round and round and finally spitting us away to the left into the outer whorls of a mighty whirlpool. As a boa constrictor swallows a deer tail-first, the terrified victim scrabbles at the ground with its front paws to escape, so our engine roared frantically as we whirled around within the sinkhole.

The black cliffs disappeared as we sunk deep within the river's bowels. Then the sinkhole closed as quickly as it had opened, spewing us violently out at a forty-five degree angle with the water boiling furiously beneath us. We were swept backwards towards the cliff. Stanley, water gushing from under his helmet, tried desperately to point the bows downstream. He failed and we were dashed violently against the rocks. The rubber hull screeched in protest and crumpled along the port side as the rubber split open.

Thrown clear of the cliffs the engine caught smoother water and we shot away into a calmer spot shouting with relief. We shook hands; both of us had considered death very close for a while. Landing downriver, we joined the others along the clifftop among some ruined Indian fishing shacks. The stench of rotten fish was overpowering.

Jack was silent and sweating profusely. The culmination of weeks of fear had come to a head. He knew it had been purely good luck that had saved us in the vortex below. He was paralysed by fear and sensibly decided not to risk the cataract. Joe was silently donning his helmet and air-bottle.

'I'll go. Jack can use my cine-camera.' It was Richard; his long black beard thrust firmly out above his gleaming frog-suit.

Joe steered with Richard up front. They shot into the very centre of the breakers and disappeared completely for long seconds. Then, over to the right, they broke clear of a whirlpool and bounced through the lower waves. Somewhere upriver, Ben loosened the C-Craft. Much later we caught it below the rapids; full of water but undamaged.

In the evening the Lillooet doctor stitched me up telling me I was extremely lucky for he had seen three good men off to the mortuary who were foolish enough to play games with the Bridge River Rapids.

Only Hell's Gate barred our way to success 200 miles further south. Once the boats were repaired we continued to Lytton where a blue-green river flows in from the east. Simon Fraser named this river after the great surveyor-explorer David Thompson whose early maps of the North West were the basis for all present-day maps of that area. Thompson never actually saw the river that bears his name and the Columbia River—which he was the first white man to descend—was lost to the United States.

From Lytton to Boston Bar the Fraser flows fast and furious through the Coastal Range to pound along a deep and gloomy gut called the Black Canyon.

We fought through successive nameless rapids hidden from the world by dizzy canyons swathed in mist and spray. We plunged down the rearing hummocks of 18-foot waves at China Bar—a rapid that caught us by surprise with its huge breakers but gave Jack back his nerve and his faith in the C-Craft. It was too late to turn back when he saw the ferocity of the China Bar waves so he clung paralysed to the tiny boat as it tossed and dived like a junk in a tropical hurricane. And afterwards, looking back, he knew that he would be able to face the final test of Hell's Gate.

An aerial tramway takes tourists from the canyon roadway downwards for 500 feet to a viewing hut above the surging water and many had come to see the British boats go through or under the waves. A mass of youngsters had the day off from school to watch the fun. Beneath them rushed the Fraser; all the water drained from 84,000 square miles of land tearing at forty knots through a gut no more than thirty-six yards wide. Thirty-four million gallons of water pass by every minute and the undercurrents are correspondingly fierce, especially so owing to the river's great depth: 175 feet at high water.

The whirlpools below Hell's Gate have sucked down 30-foot inflatable boats, folding them in half the better to accommodate them.

As we struggled through the Gate, Bryn's costly waterproof camera snapped free from its fixtures and sank. The other boats careened through without mishap; Jack and Joe in the C-Craft dwarfed by the great exploding breakers.

A mile below the Gate, we came near to disaster in a vicious rapid no one had warned us of. Further on at the narrows called Sailor's Bar we slithered through saw-tooth rocks where a year before a 30-foot rubber raft carrying five soldiers from Chilliwack army base had capsized. All the men had lifejackets and only one drowned.

High above the river rears the grey steel span of Alexandra Bridge close to the spot where the original Spuzzum Bridge with its hand-spun steel cables once rumbled beneath the wagonwheels of the goldrush. Here too Simon Fraser paused after portaging along the precarious Indian cliff trail of vine ropes and narrow ledges. Close by Spuzzum he was able to continue by river in dug-out canoes.

Evening brushed the orange glades of the upper valleys a thousand feet above us. Autumn glowed about the river as it cleft the last confining ramparts of the canyon. A bare and solitary island, the Lady Franklin Rock, split the river and beyond it, in a gentler land, there curled the lazy smoke of Yale where we landed.

The little town nestles close by the high-water mark, despite a long history of floods, looking very like the paintings of itself in 1858 when the first fine sternwheeler arrived. It is not difficult, sitting by the Fraser's sandy shore, to picture the soft plunk of the paddle wheel, the cheers of the hopeful miners, the tinkling gaiety from the old crap 'n faro hall called Panama Lil's with its crystal chandeliers, champagne, and German dancing girls.

The slender fur-laden canoes of the buckskin-clad voyageurs had crunched against this same shingle beach and—by the old town hall—the first British law on the mainland of British Columbia was proclaimed.

After Yale, we moved through a rich rolling land of farm and industry and at Agassiz noticed the first tidal influences on the river. Four days later the Fraser split into three wide channels below the city of New Westminster, once the capital but now a mere suburb of sprawling Vancouver; sprawling, but very beautiful in its setting of snow-clad mountains and caressed by warm breezes from the Strait of Georgia, tempered by the warm Japanese Current.

A sea mist crept over the Delta marshes and we nosed cautiously west into Pacific waters until, clear of hidden shoals, our route lay south to Point Roberts. A fog horn sounded through the murk; a dead, clammy sound and many times we lost each other and all sense of direction in the fog. But Ben Usher had friends in the Delta police who sent a launch to help us find our way. At four o'clock the police helmsman, checking his chart, called across through the thick yellow haze.

'This is it, folks, you done it. We're in Yank territory now.'

A ragged cheer rose from the three scruffy boats, eight bearded wind-tanned faces creased in wide tired grins, and Richard Robinson delved in his mummy-bag to produce three kingsize bottles of champagne. It was not Moët et Chandon Dom Perignon 59 but it was very welcome.

Bubbly flowed liberally in the gloom and an unholy chorus sounded through the mist led by the dulcet tones of Bryn the Celt.

The champagne finished off all remaining sense of direction so we clung like limpets to the launch. Some while later a brine-crusted jetty loomed ahead and the sea slapped softly on a gentle beach.

There were many people with flashing lights and cameras, a US ranger with a drooping Stars 'n Stripes and a Mountie with a Maple Leaf. Ginnie and Sarah were there and a host of well-wishers.

We had crossed the 49th Parallel; many cold green leagues from the Nahanni and the Arctic Circle.

In the days that followed, before the RAF sent planes to take us home, we arrived officially at English Bay in Vancouver, a Union Jack flying from the stern, to be welcomed by the people of the city. The alderman presented us with medals on the beach and appointed us Honorary Aldermen of Vancouver. An expatriot Briton with tears in his eyes told us he'd been following our journey for months in his newspaper and now felt just like he had on the day of Dunkirk: 'real proud to be British'.

Telegrams of congratulations came from the Army back in Britain and the High Commissioner in Ottawa. The Trade Commission had our boats and equipment whisked off to a demonstration and a series of exhibitions. Many sales and orders followed including the sale of the two RFD boats and the portable canoes to Vancouver dealers. The little C-Craft was removed by the Dunlop agent for a CBC television film and for Boat Shows in Toronto and Earl's Court. Many months later it was returned to me for use on other expeditions.

Vancouver is a city of over one million people, although it is only a century old. We lectured to its universities, to over forty schools and at civic functions: to know about your country is to be concerned about its future. British Columbia is certainly one of the most unspoilt regions in the world but it is also one of the richest in raw materials. As such, it is a natural showcase to the world, reflecting the position of the struggle everywhere between those who strive to bolster the living standards of our generation and those who fight for the environmental rights of our grandchildren.

Richard and Paul returned to other missions with the BBC, Bryn joined the select group of the world's top photographers known as Magnum, and Ben Usher is now the Constable at Withernsea in East Yorkshire. Joe, Jack and Stanley are back with their regiments though all three have muttered dark threats about emigrating to British Columbia. At Christmas Jack telephoned from war-torn Belfast to say how relaxing life was there after the rigours and tension of 'the river life'.

Ginnie and I sent Skook a thick English blanket as we had promised, only to learn later that a great fire had come by night below Terminus Mountain to the Kingdom of Skook and that all his possessions had been burnt, even the medals of which he had been so proud—but the old man had escaped with his life. The great elements of Fire and Earth, Air and Water still hold sway, if not untrammelled, in the wild Rocky Mountains and north to the Arctic in the land of Nahanni, 'somewhere over there and beyond'.

Acknowledgments

The Expedition was made possible only through the generous help and hospitality of a number of persons and organisations. Without their support the venture would not have taken place and we are extremely grateful to our sponsors and friends in Britain and Canada.

We wish to thank:
Colonel Mike Gannon
Rupert Hodges of British Petroleum
Keith Kent and Brian Sperring of the Rover Co. Ltd
Duckhams Oils
Curt Lammerich of C-Craft Ltd

Army Strategic Command
AT1
Major J. Appleton
Colonel Bateman, RSDG
Major Joe Bergner
Lt-Colonel Micky Blacklock, RSDG
Major J. Blashford-Snell, MBE
CFHQ, Ottawa
Lt-General M. R. Dare, DSO, CD
Spencer Eade
Major T. Egremont-Lee
Major Fraser, AT Films
Wing Commander George
Sqn Ldr Girdwood

ACKNOWLEDGMENTS

George Greenfield
Harry Harrod
Major Bill Haynes, RSDG
Major Hedges of Instow Underwater Research Dept
Capt G. C. Hopkins
The 'Jo's, Ruth and others at the Main Building, MOD
Mr McLeod of BC House
The Natural History Museum, Zoology & Palaeontology Depts
Colonel Ken Neely
Capt Ron Patterson, RSDG
Major R. Peel
Rear Admiral Stirling
Staff Sgt Taylor of Instow Underwater Research Dept
RAF Transport Command
Major Brian Roberts
Major Ian Robertson
Richard Fiennes, MA, MRCVS & the Royal Zoological Society of
    London
The Librarians of the Royal Geographical Society
Major Stephen Stopford, MBE, RSDG
Major Waite, ATLO
Colonel Buster Wilson-Brown
John Wright

Bob Angus
Brigadier & Mrs Arnold-Edwards
Joe Bishop
Mrs Gordon Bowes
Robert & Helen Brown
Stan Bridcutt of Watson Lake Flying Services Inc
L. D. Byrne, British Trade Commission
Canadian Freightways
Chapman Transport Ltd
Renee Chipman
Jim Close of Watson Lake Flying Services Inc
Jack Coleman of Carrier Lumber Ltd
Chief Coles of Chilliwack Garrison
Ed Cooper
Rex Davidson and the staff of West Coast Transmission
Skook Davidson
Bob Depree of Woodwards

Brian Doke
Frank Dolan
Hughie Dunlop and the staff of Hell's Gate
Dennis Elsom and the Police and Corporation of Delta
Doctor John Ferries
Moira Farrow
John T. Fowler of BP Oils Canada Ltd
Peter & Jane Fowler
George Galicz of the Surrey Zoo
Bill Galt, Mr Norris, and the staff of the *Sun*
John & Julie Garry
The Govt of NWT
Gulf Oil representatives in BC
Harry & Frankie Hansen
Cog Harrington of the Charles Hotel, Boston Bar
Doctor Alan High
The owner of Highland Glen
Mr J. C. Hollies
Lorne Hunter
Derek Lukin Johnston, FCA
Ron Jones of the BC Timber Land Service
Georgie Keddell
Douglas Erskine-Kellie
Doctor & Mrs Tony Kenyan
Jack Klein of MacMillan Bloedel Ltd
Capt Magray of Search & Rescue, Vancouver Island
Alec McMeekin of the Greys
Glen Mayes
Mr Marshall, Bank of Montreal
Father Mary
Ken Melville of Tudya Lake Lodge
Baptiste Matoux
Ken McGee
The McCooks of Fox Lake
John Mohammed
T. F. Moon
John Miller of the HBC Fort Liard
Ma Murray
Dave Milne
George Nelms
Northern Thunderbird Airlines – Ed McPherson, Dave Whelan, L. Ritchie, and the pilots

H. J. Pascoe of BLMC Ltd Vancouver
Mr Raymond M. Patterson
Ian Patterson of BLMC Ontario
Mr & Mrs Alan F. Pierce
The Citizens of Prince George
The RCMP at: Fort Liard, Fort Nelson, Watson Lake, Pointed Mntn,
    Attlin, Prince George, Mackenzie, Fort St John, Boston Bar, Summit
    Lake, Williams Lake & Lytton. Also the Forest Service and Fish &
    Game Depts in those regions
Majors Ray & Hovercroft of Chilliwack Garrison
Luke Reisebeck
Mr & Mrs Karl Rieche
Wayne Scott of BLMC Prince George
Barbara Sehmer & family
Drucie Stavdal & Chris
Bill Steele of Kitsilano Marine Ltd
M. G. Stoner of Penaroyya (Canada) Ltd
George Streeper
Swede Stromquist
The men of Texas Gulf Sulphur: Nahanni detachment
Major & Mrs Douglas Tobler
Mr & Mrs Dick Turner & Don Turner
Malcolm Turnbull & the staff of the *Province*
Bill & Pat Van Somers
Jim Van Somers
Steve Villars, Len, & the pilots of Northern Air Services
Bud & Lois Ward
Stan & Isabel Weston
Leo Wilkinson
Mr & Mrs Windrum
Dick & Shelley Wright

Dennis & Barry Bate of D. Dixon Bate Ltd
W. R. R. Price of Batchelor Foods Ltd
Bostik Ltd
W. B. Wilkinson of Bovril Group Marketing Ltd
R. H. Cornford of Brooke Bond Oxo Ltd
William Stirling of James Buchanan & Co. Ltd
Sqn Ldr J. A. Cook of Burndept Electronics Ltd
Cadbury's Chocolate Ltd
Ken Catt

ACKNOWLEDGMENTS

K. S. Meakin of Ciba-Geigy (UK) Ltd
Crown Cup Coffee
Dunlop Rubber Co. Ltd
FPT Ltd
Fray Bentos Corned Beef
Miss P. F. McClintock of Glaxo Ltd
N. P. Cutcliffe of H. J. Heinz Ltd
Hodder & Stoughton Ltd
Holland & Holland Ltd
Husky of Tostock Ltd
Kendall's Mint Cake
Labgear Ltd (Pye Group)
Lillywhites of Piccadilly
Lockhart Equipment Ltd
Eddie Hawkins of Marlow Ropes Ltd
G. Harris of Mars Chocolate Ltd
R. Hampton of the Metal Box Co. Ltd
J. A. Ridgewell of Mitchell Cotts Service Ltd
The New Zipper Co.
Chris Hawksworth of The Northern Wild Water Centre
The management & staff of *The Observer*
Pains-Wessex Ltd
Edgar Lewy of Philart Productions Ltd, 11 Bermondsey St, SE1 (Special
    expedition philatelic covers available)
Peter Cox & Harry Collins of Rank Audio-Visual Ltd
J. Crerar of Racal Electronics Ltd
The management & staff of RFD GQ Ltd
Commander Cairns & Lieutenant Stogdon of the RNLI
Rolex
Patricia Lotery of Saward Baker & Co. Ltd
Sellotape Products Ltd
Bill Nelson of Schermuly Ltd
Shippams Meat Pastes
Silver Bell Cow & Gate Cheese
Standard Brands Royal Instant Drinking Chocolate
Trevor A. Smith of Subaqua Services Ltd
Sutherlands Spreads
Joan Jackson of Tupperware Ltd
Tyne Canoes Ltd
Mrs P. Golding of Unigate Ltd
E. J. Boote of Unilever Exports Ltd
Whitbread & Co. Ltd

ACKNOWLEDGMENTS

Wilkinson Sword Ltd
P. A. Savage of the Wrigley Co. Ltd
Betty Law of Yardley International Ltd

There are many others who helped the expedition who are not named above but to whom our thanks are no less due.

Bibliography

Begg, Alexander. *History of British Columbia from its Earliest Discovery to the Present Time*. Toronto, Briggs, 1894.

Black, Samuel. *A journal of a Voyage from Rocky Mountain Portage in Peace River to the sources of the Finlay's branch and Northwestward in 1824*. Ed. by E. E. Rich, London, Hudson Bay Record Society, 1955.

Bowes, Gordon E., ed. *Peace River Chronicles*. Vancouver, Prescott Pub. Co., 1963.

Burpee, Lawrence J. 'A Road To Alaska', *Canadian Geographical Journal*, November 1940.

Creighton, Donald Grant. *Dominion of the North, a History of Canada*. Houghton 1944.

de Hulle, Emma – Evelyn E. Cunningham. *Bridge River Gold*. Vancouver, Evergreen Press Ltd

Fleming, Sir Sandford. *Report of Progress on the Explorations and Surveys of the Canadian Pacific Railway up to January 1874*. Ottawa, MacLean, Rogers & Co., 1874.

Futcher, Winifred M. *The Great North Road To Cariboo*. Vancouver, Wrigley, 1938.

Haworth, Paul L. 'To the Quadacha Country and Mount Lloyd George', *Scribner's Magazine*. Vol. 67, June 1920.

Hedley, M. S. and Holland, Stuart S. *Reconnaissance in the Area of Turnagain and Upper Kechika Rivers, Northern B.C.* BC Department of Mines, Bulletin No. 12, 1941.

Hutchinson, Bruce. *The Fraser*. Toronto, Clarke, Irvin & Co. Ltd, 1950.

Hacking, Norman R. 'British Columbia Steamboat Days 1870–1883', *British Columbia Historical Quarterly*, October 1944.

Howay, F. W. *British Columbia, The Making of a Province*. Toronto, Ryerson, 1928.

Jenness, Diamond. *The Sekani Indians of British Columbia*. Bulletin No. 84, Anthropological Series No. 20, National Museum of Canada, Ottawa, 1937.

Keddell, Georgina M. *Muskeg Maze*. Fort St John, 1963.

Leacock, Stephen. *Adventures of the Far North*. Glasgow, Brook, 1914.

MacGregor, James G. *The Land of Twelve-Foot Davis – A History of the Peace River Country*. Edmonton, 1952.

MacKay, Douglas. *The Honourable Company, a History of the Hudson's Bay Company*. Indianapolis, Bobbs-Merrill, 1936.

MacKenzie, Sir Alexander. *Voyages From Montreal Through The Continent of America To The Frozen And Pacific Oceans in 1789 and 1793*. Toronto, Courier Press, 1911.

McNaughton, Margaret. *Overland To Cariboo*. Toronto, Briggs, 1896.

McConnell, Richard George. *Report on an Exploration of the Finlay and Omineca Rivers*. Canada Geological Survey, Annual Report (new series), 5.7.1894.

Moodie, J. D. *Edmonton to the Yukon*. Report of the North West Police, 1898.

Ormsby, Margaret A. *British Columbia, a History*. Vancouver, The MacMillan Company of Canada Ltd, 1958.

Patterson, R. M. *Finlay's River*. Toronto, Macmillan, 1968.

Patterson, R. M. *Dangerous River*. Toronto, Macmillan, 1968.

Porter, McKenzie. 'The Bizarre Mystery of B.C.'s Champagne Safari' (the Bedaux Expedition), *MacLean's Magazine*. November 10, 1956.

Rainee, Froelich. 'Alaskan Highway, An Engineering Epic', *National Geographical Magazine*. February 1943.

Rickard, T. A. *Historical Backgrounds of British Columbia*. Vancouver, Wrigley, 1948.

Robertson, W. Fleet. *Report* 1908, BC Department of Mines, 1909.

Scholefield, E. O. S. *British Columbia From The Earliest Times To The Present*. Vol. 1, Vancouver, S. J. Clarke Publishing Company.

Selwyn, Alfred C. *Report of Exploration in British Columbia, Canada*. Geological Survey, Report 1875–76, Ottawa, 1877.

Swannell, Frank C. *Report on Exploration of Finlay and Ingenika Valleys. Cassiar District season 1914*. BC Sessional Papers. Third Session, Thirteenth Parliament. Session 1915. Report to the Minister of Lands for the year ending 31st December 1914.

Swannell, Frank C. 'Ninety Years Later', in the *Beaver Magazine*. Spring 1956.

Vallance, J. D. *Untrodden Ways*. Victoria, Hebden Printing Company Ltd.

Wade, M. S. *Overlanders of '62*. Victoria, Banfield, 1931.

Wallace, J. N. 'The Explorer of Finlay River in 1824', in the *Canadian Historical Review*, 1928.

Index

217

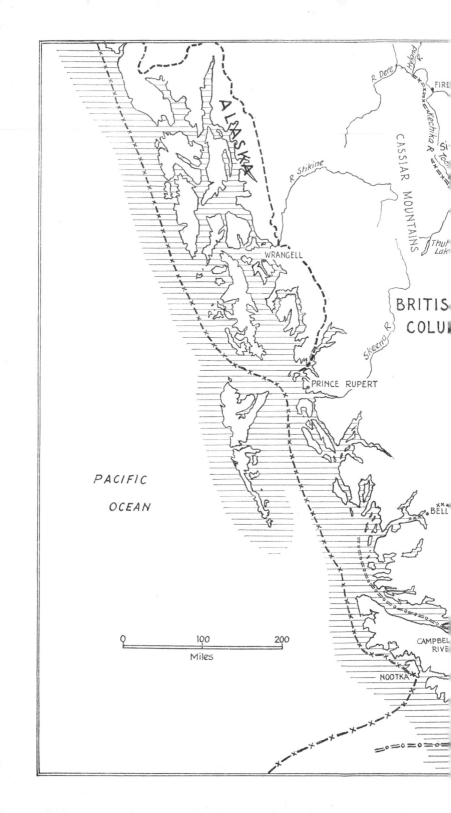